Praise for
Stop Waiting for It to Get Easier:
Create Your Dream Business Now!

Ready, fire, aim - it's the essential and much needed advice Jim Palmer dispenses in his latest book. But he isn't simply advocating throwing caution to the wind. Instead, he masterfully provides two key ingredients today's entrepreneurs desperately need to succeed – solid business strategies and inspiration to find the courage to take action and make your dreams come true now. If you have a great idea, are considering entrepreneurship but need the guidance and push to make your dream a reality, *Stop Waiting* is a must read!

> – Adam Urbanski,
> The Millionaire Marketing Mentor®
> Founder and CEO, TheMarketingMentors.com

If more budding entrepreneurs and visionaries read Jim Palmer's book, *Stop Waiting for It to Get Easier – Create Your Dream Business Now,* then more successful business owners would exist today! I couldn't agree more with Jim's advice, and I think this book is a must read for anyone with a dream of creating their first business – or making the one they have work better! The information in *Stop Waiting* could make the difference between sitting on the side line watching everyone else get successful … and being a huge success yourself.

> –Melanie Benson Strick
> America's Leading Small Business Optimizer
> www.successconnections.com

I was honored to write the foreword for Jim's second book, *Stick Like Glue*. At the time I wrote "Jim Palmer is one of the greatest teachers to provide you with techniques and strategies to take you to an entirely new level of understanding and success in your business." Well, Jim has done it again! His latest book, *Stop Waiting for It to Get Easier – Create Your Dream Business Now,* is likely exactly what you need to hear to get your business to the next level. I'm also hoping that thousands more will read this book because I know it will cause many with the dream of becoming an entrepreneur, to finally "Stop Waiting" and take action now.

> –Lee Milteer
> Best Selling Author, Professional speaker and
> Intuitive Business Coach
> www.milteer.com

Stop! There's no need to do any more thinking, pondering, or wondering "What if ...?" In Jim's latest book, he's given you a clear path to the most important ingredient in any successful business – action. In addition to this outstanding 'kick in the pants' that we all need, Jim provides facts, tips and success strategies on how to easily and cost-effectively dominate your market and virtually eliminate any competition you have, and position your business as the number one choice for the products and services you sell. *Stop Waiting* is the perfect antidote to inaction!

–Martin Howey, Founder and Chief Executive Officer
Top Line Business Solutions
www.toplinebusinesssolutions.com

Stop Waiting, Jim Palmer's latest and best book yet, is a not about theory or fuzzy business thinking. In Zen terms, all we have is today, and this book is about actually taking your dream to create your own business from thought to reality... right now. This action plan of a book is designed to take the newbie entrepreneur from dreamer to business owner and the existing business owner from goal setter to achiever. Get it. Read it. Do it. You'll never look back.

–Dave Frees
Persuasion and Influence Master,
Attorney, and Author
www.successtechnologies.com

Jim Palmer has done the aspiring entrepreneur a huge favor with his latest book. You'll find pithy and practical advice for getting started, creating value and making money. Make sure you check out *Stop Waiting* and the Success Tips and Gems sections at the end of each chapter! Buy it. Study it. Implement the suggestions and succeed!

–Mike Capuzzi
Direct Marketing Strategist
www.MikeCapuzzi.com

If you've been on the fence about "going for it" with your own business – just DO IT! Jim provides a decision-making blueprint to help you choose and run the right business for you. Your business should support your lifestyle, and Jim's no nonsense way of delivering this hard hitting and practical how-to information is a must read. I wish I had this when I started my first business!

–Stephanie Frank
Best Selling Author, *The Accidental Millionaire*
www.StephanieFrank.com

Are you an entrepreneur? Maybe you're a "wantreprenenuer" (someone wanting to start a business). If you're struggling with challenges in your existing business or wanting to start a business but don't know where to look, you've found your answers here with Jim Palmer's book. *Stop Waiting for It to Get*

Easier is more of a straight talking, personal session with Jim than a book on entrepreneurship. His motivational stories and examples will light a fire within you and get you moving! Don't wait any longer start right now!

–Michelle Prince
Best-Selling Author, Zig Ziglar Motivational Speaker,
Productivity & Publishing Expert
www.MichellePrince.com

Stop Waiting for It to Get Easier is the "kick-in-the-pants" most entrepreneurs and small business owners who are waiting for the right time to act really need! The thing I have grown to love about Jim Palmer and this latest book is he doesn't sugar coat the fact that success takes hard work, the time is never going to be just right, and most of all, success and money love speed. Jim advises us now is the best time to start your new business venture; the economy isn't an excuse, it's a great reason to burn your boats, so you can't turn back. Believe in your idea with conviction and you will make significant, measurable progress toward success. Take action now, you won't regret it!

–Paul D. Guyon,
Traverse City, Michigan
www.paulguyon.com

Jim Palmer has done it again with his new book, *Stop Waiting for It to Get Easier*. Instead of waiting for a "return to normal," this book is all about creating one's own economy, finding a problem to solve and stepping up to the plate by starting a new business or bringing life to an existing one that needs revitalization. Through his own story of overcoming a mid-career lay-off and surviving cancer, Jim is able to inspire others to look at life's challenges as opportunities rather than adversity and show why today's economic downturn is the best climate to affirm change and transform your own life to live with purpose and passion. Stop Waiting! Get this book now!

–Dr. David Phelps, D.D.S.
North America's Leading Authority on Professional Practice Freedom
www.DiscoverFreedomHere.com

Jim has nailed it again with his great new book. If you are looking for a practical, timely and authentic book on what it really takes to succeed in business, then get this book! Let his wisdom and knowledge help guide you to greater business success and profits!

–Tony Rubleski
President, Mind Capture Group
www.MindCaptureGroup.com

A few years ago, I asked Jim Palmer to be my business coach. That year, I had some of the best results ever. Why? Two reasons:
1. Jim saw opportunities that were right in front of me that I could not see for myself and he helped me exploit them for maximum profit.

2. He made me take action on those opportunities immediately and report back to him the results. The timing wasn't perfect. I just did what he told me to do. I didn't wait until it was perfect. I got stuff done and fortunately, experienced great results.

My actions and results were all inspired by Jim's coaching and advice. In his new book, *Stop Waiting for It to Get Easier – Create Your Dream Business Now,* Jim helps you get rid of any excuses that might come to mind when starting a business and gets you to see why taking action now is a lot easier and more profitable in the end. Jim says, and I agree, "Bad economic conditions are never an excuse not to get started. In fact, just the opposite. It's a great reason to get started." Read this book and listen to Jim's advice like I did and "stop waiting and get going" on the road to finally reaching your goals and dreams now."

–Craig A. Valine
Marketing Performance Strategist
www.NoBSCraigValine.com

Stop Waiting is truly an entrepreneur's business plan, containing everything you need to lay the foundations for a wildly successful business. Just open the book to any page, read the first thing your eyes focus upon, learn the lesson and take the action.

Time and time again, Jim Palmer has said, a "sale" does not automatically equal a "customer." How right he is! The chapter on "Types of Revenue" will make you think critically about making your business profitable and fill in gaps you did not even know existed.

Regardless of where you start, you'll recoup your investment in *Stop Waiting* about 5 minutes after you start reading.

–Adam Hommey
Host, Business Creators' Radio Show
www.businesscreatorsradioshow.com

I can relate to what Jim describes as "Stuck in a Rut." Fortunately, by the grace of God, I took what I love and was really good at and created my own dream business. It wasn't easy, still isn't. But now I am able to raise my new baby girl at home, while creating my own business working for profits instead of a paycheck!

–Sherrie Sokolowski
Founder of SLS Event Planning and Consulting, LLC
slseventplanning.com

Starting a business is a lot like having children. Both beg the "When is the best time?" question. If you wait until you can afford either, you won't... ever. Read Jim Palmer's *Stop Waiting for It to Get Easier* and act now to give life to your business idea. That way your kids will have a job.

–Dr. Joey Faucette, Work Positive in a Negative World
www.listentolife.org

If you could have ONE secret weapon for your success, Jim Palmer's *Stop Waiting for It to Get Easier – Create Your Dream Business Now* is THE secret weapon you've been looking for. Whether you are a beginning entrepreneur, or an experienced business owner, Jim exposes his own successes and failures and gives you the unvarnished truth about the real business world. Counter-intuitive and innovative, Jim gets you thinking bigger, operating smarter and making sure you are profitable from the start! Use this book like a workbook. Mark it up, dog ear the pages and soak up the wisdom. I wish I had this book in my hands 30 years ago!

–Brad Szollose
21st Century Change Agent
www.LiquidLeadership.com

Regardless of where you are in your entrepreneurial journey, this book is for you! It offers some terrific wisdom for the person thinking of starting a new venture, as well invaluable reminders for the seasoned entrepreneur. In either case, the contents of this book will help you accelerate your success.

–Nile Nickel
LinkedInFocus.com

Burn the boats! Cut the rope! It's time to go all in with your business idea. In *Stop Waiting for It to Get Easier*, Jim Palmer is going to give you the permission you want to get started and then a kind kick in the pants to make sure you get going. This book gives you the HOW and WHY you need to move ahead NOW.

–Lori Saitz,
Appreciation Marketing Expert
www.ZenRabbit.com

In *Stop Waiting for It to Get Easier – Create Your Dream Business Now*, Jim Palmer attacks the NUMBER ONE issue facing all would be entrepreneurs, small business owners, struggling entrepreneurs, and, quite frankly, ever person I've ever met and that issue is FEAR. I waited a decade to start Top Practices because I was working on my plan (read: too chicken to do it). I thought my big corporate job with the big paycheck and benefits package was a safety net I just couldn't live without. When I finally did take the plunge, I discovered that what I thought was a safety net was actually a cage. I was really just like a piece of furniture at that big company, and I had a high executive level position. I was told what I would earn and how often I could take a vacation. Now I live my live on my terms. Period. Jim is so right, if I knew then what Jim teaches in this book, I could've started at least 10 years before I did. Congratulations to Jim Palmer on another essential book for business owners. I'm proud to call Jim Palmer a friend and colleague and that is why he is the Keynote Speaker at the Top Practices Annual Summit this year.

–Rem Jackson, President and CEO
Top Practices, LLC
www.TopPractices.com

Do you know a friend, colleague, or perhaps a group
that would enjoy and benefit from the information and
strategies in this book?
If so, we're happy to extend the following volume discounts!

Stop Waiting for It to Get Easier:
Create Your Dream Business Now

$19.95 U.S.

Special Quantity Discounts
5-20 Books - $16.95
21-50 Books - $13.95
51-100 Books - $11.95
101-250 Books - $8.95
251-500 Books - $6.95

Call or e-mail today to order bulk quantities
610-458-2047
guru@TheNewsletterGuru.com

Stop Waiting for It to Get Easier: Create Your Dream Business Now!

By Jim Palmer
The Newsletter Guru

With a Foreword by Kevin Harrington

CUSTOM NEWSLETTERS, INC.

Stop Waiting for It to Get Easier:
Create Your Dream Business Now!

Published by Success Advantage Publishing
64 East Uwchlan Ave.
P.O. Box 231
Exton, PA 19341

ISBN: 978-0615890074

Cover design by Jim Saurbaugh, JS Graphic Design

This book is dedicated to my family,
Stephanie, Nick, Steve, Jessica, and Amanda.

·

Table of Contents

Chapter Fourteen:

Foreword

Now is the time to act.

On an early episode of ABC's Shark Tank, entrepreneur Rebecca Rescate stepped up to face the sharks and immediately played a video of her cat running into her bathroom and doing its business – in the toilet! All five sharks burst into laughter at what we had just seen!

Rebecca is the developer of CitiKitty®, a program that teaches cats how to use a toilet rather than a litter box. At that time, CitiKitty® was on track to do $350k in sales, and altogether, CitiKitty® had generated sales of $1.4 million dollars. Not a bad start to be sure, but Rebecca knew that CitiKitty® had enormous potential, and she came to Shark Tank seeking both additional working capital and expertise to help her take her business to the next level. She knew that now was the time to act.

Rebecca's story contains a few important entrepreneurial lessons. First, she saw a need and wasted no time in creating a unique solution. Then, after having some marginal success, she grabbed the bull by the horns one more time and sought the help she knew needed to help her business be as successful and profitable as she knew it could be. In essence, Rebecca, like many other entrepreneurs, embraced the mantra that I live by: now is the time to act!

In many ways, Rebecca's story is what entrepreneurship is all about. She had an idea, that idea became a dream and eventually a product. Most importantly, when it really counted, Rebecca was not afraid to step up to the plate and take a shot at creating a better life for her and her family. If you have a dream and vision, now is the time to act, or as Jim says, "Stop waiting for it to get easier!"

As Jim's book wonderfully illustrates with story after story, successful businesses are created every day, no matter what the economy or other outside market conditions may be. The truth is there is never a 'perfect' time to start a business, so why not start now?

As I've demonstrated countless times in my businesses as well as working with several other highly successful business owners, I believe that entrepreneurs who move swiftly and boldly from idea into action, delivering value to the marketplace, will ultimately succeed.

In my book, *Act Now-How I Turn Ideas into Million Dollar Products,* I share how I was earning $2000 to $4000 per month as a 16 year old when most of my friends were earning $1.60 an hour flipping burgers! There is no better example of what's possible when you switch your mindset from one of trading your time for money and earning a paycheck to one that creates value for consumers and, in doing so, builds a business and earns profits.

I'm often asked what holds some people back from taking the plunge and starting a business. Fear plays a big part in the hesitation, but as much as fear can be a deterrent to action, it can also serve as motivation to get you *into* action – and outside your comfort zone – where most growth occurs.

Early in my career, I noticed that I had some 'fear issues' regarding selling. I was very fortunate to be able to get some amazing on-the-job training from one of the best salespeople I've ever known. I not only watched and learned his techniques, I began implementing them, and low and behold, I too got very good at sales. If there's only one skill every successful entrepreneur should be great at it's how to close a sale. You can have the best product and logo in the world, but without sales, you simply have no business.

As you consider starting a business, or perhaps growing an existing business, I want to encourage you to become curious. This might sound strange, but all of the successful entrepreneurs that I know and work with have what I often refer to as 'curiosity overload.' Highly successful entrepreneurs have an insatiable appetite for knowledge – always looking for the slight edge that can take them to the next level. You should be reading several books a month, attending live events and seminars, and meeting with other entrepreneurs to learn what works in their businesses.

There's another reason that the best time to act is now, and that's because the world is changing rapidly. In fact, the world is changing so fast that if you don't move on your idea, it may be outdated by the time you muster the courage to do so!

You can and should learn a great deal from this book. Jim has not only pulled together some great success stories from big businesses you no doubt are familiar with but also some stories from new entrepreneurs who have recently started or expanded their businesses. They are all inspirational, and if you glean from them what I did, you'll see that they all decided that now is the time to act.

Finally, if you feel that life is simply presenting you with too many challenges right now, I believe Jim's story of starting his business broke, after overcoming long-term unemployment, and a scary experience with cancer will give you some inspiration. After being unemployed for 13 months, Jim was told by his doctors that he had cancer… it literally dropped him to his knees. Jim was facing the challenge of his lifetime, but he confronted the cancer just like he would an entrepreneurial problem. Jim worked hard to overcome the problem – getting the best advice, seeking out the best doctors, and monitoring programs… and he's been cancer-free for 12 years. Jim didn't allow his incredible challenge to deter him. In fact, he used it to get in gear, embracing 'now is the time to act' thinking.

When Jim sent me a copy of the manuscript for this book, I not only agreed with his premise and main message of the book, which he captures so efficiently in the title, I also knew immediately that I wanted to be part of it. Like Jim, I believe that entrepreneurs are not only what makes our country great, but small business is what drives our economy and will be what ultimately lifts our fledgling economy out of the ditch. So I encourage you to Stop Waiting for it to Get Easier, and Start Creating Your Dream Business Now!

Allow me to close by sharing a phrase that I always carry with me on a small card. I hope that it inspires and encourages you as much as it does me. *"Life's battles don't always go to the fastest or the strongest – sooner or later those who win are those who think they can."*

Kevin Harrington, Chairman of As Seen on TV, Inc. and former investor "Shark" on ABC's Shark Tank

Here's Kevin Harrington (left) pictured on the set of Shark Tank with Kevin O'Leary, Daymond John, Barbara Corcoran, and Robert Herjavec.

Preface

This book is specifically for two groups of people. First, it's for those people who have long had a dream of starting a business – being an entrepreneur, controlling their own destiny but just waiting for the right time to get started. Secondly, it is for those entrepreneurs and small business owners who've already started but have not yet reached their dreams or goals for the business. Perhaps you've yet to break the six-figure mark, or you already hit six figures but are waiting for the right time to launch phase two. And whether that means launching a new program, product, location, or simply implementing an aggressive marketing campaign to propel your growth and profitability forward, you're waiting for the best and, perhaps, safest time to do it.

If you fit into either of these two scenarios, you'll notice a common theme. Both are *waiting for the right time* to act. To be candid and rather blunt (something my coaching clients know me to be), they're actually waiting for the courage, or the guts, or to get off the dime and seize the moment.

While you will find in these pages literally dozens of lessons, tips, and nuggets of wisdom, the ONE single message that I want you to hear and glean from reading this book is that NOW is the time to act. There is no better time than now to act smartly but boldly, and either start your business or take your existing business to the next level. As with my other books, I will not waste your time with some pie in the sky philosophy or grand choruses of "you can do it!"

Instead, I will share not only the real world examples of my life and career, but I'll also share some stories – evidence – from some more well-known names. To start, I'm going to give you the background you need to help inspire you and get you ready to jump in along with historical examples (stories of entrepreneurs who are well-known *now* that will certainly surprise you as well as inspire you) – evidence that shows why now is the best time to launch your business or take the next step in the business you're already running. Next, you'll also find at the end of each chapter, some entrepreneurial wisdom and business building nuggets to both inspire you and help get you ready to really succeed – the "nuts and bolts" business information that I think is *most* important for any aspiring or new entrepreneur.

By the way, if you enjoy these nuggets and gems, I invite you to connect with me on social media. You'll easily find me on Facebook, LinkedIn, and Google Plus, and I share these gems almost daily!

Finally, I've included interviews of five entrepreneurs – real-world stories of others who all started or aggressively expanded their businesses within the last three years. As usual with my books, you'll also find handy recaps at the conclusion of each chapter along with additional bonus success tips. All of this is, as I mentioned, for one purpose: To encourage you, enlighten you, and most importantly, motivate you to take action and seize the moment.

In the early 1980s, I was the manager of a bicycle store. As jobs go, it was a fun job, especially for a young twenty-something to have. I was a cyclist myself, and I got to ride to work and then 'play' with all the new bikes and accessories. I was the embodiment of the expression, "a kid in a candy store!"

Little did I know that those early, 'fun' working years would also provide the very foundation of the business success principles that I use in my businesses today and that I teach to the many entrepreneurs and small business owners that I coach in my mastermind groups and privately.

The economy in the early 80s was still dealing with what is commonly referred to as the Carter recession. At the time, the nation was gripped with double-digit inflation, double-digit unemployment, and double-digit interest rates. This was not a 'business friendly' environment, to be sure, but thanks to that 'training by fire,' it's where I cut my teeth as a retailer, as a smart marketer, and as a successful businessman. I owe much of my values and success to learning how to market, sell, and lead a business during really tough times. I sometimes wonder where I'd be or what I'd be doing had the economy been roaring and the only thing I had to figure out was when to open the door! But I digress.

Running a small business during this severe recession was challenging to say the least. We were seeing fewer and fewer customers every day, and that obviously had a real impact on our sales and bottom line. But in my youth and perhaps naiveté, I was determined to grow this business with the tools and resources I had. I'm not sure who said it first, but I remember a radio talk show host in Philadelphia at the time who ended every show with this phrase: "Tough times don't last, tough people do!" It was kind of a call to arms! I took it as "Buck up, stop complaining, and get to work!"

Whether it was this call to arms or my youthful exuberance, I began to implement some creative marketing and business growth strategies that worked amazingly well for this bike shop, and we did start to grow.

I've written about many of these marketing and growth strategies in three of my previous books, *The Magic of Newsletter Marketing – The Secret to More Profits and Customers for Life; Stick Like Glue – How to Create and Everlasting Bond with Your Customers So They Stay Longer, Spend More, and Refer More;* and *The Fastest Way to Higher Profits – 19 Immediate Profit Enhancing Strategies That You Can Use Today.* I encourage you to check them out at www.SuccessAdvantagePublishing.com or at Amazon. They're all available in either paperback or Kindle.

The reason I've decided to write *this* book at *this* time is that once again our country is dealing with a sluggish economy, and I see many entrepreneurs and small business owners struggling and, rightly or wrongly, laying some of the blame on our current economic challenges.

When times are tough, entrepreneurs have two choices. They can 'hunker down' and operate their business much more conservatively – essentially pulling in their horns and, in some cases, sticking their heads in the sand until things return to normal or somehow in their eyes get better. I do not believe this is a good growth strategy. When you pull in your horns and cut staff, marketing, inventory, available hours, etc., this more often than not becomes a self-fulfilling prophecy and business does, in fact, begin to decline.

The second choice is to recognize that no matter what the global or national economic environment is doing, entrepreneurs who provide massive value, delivered to their customers, clients, and patients with what I call 'World Class Service' – and market their businesses with 'Smart Marketing and Business Building Ideas[TM]' – can experience significant growth in their businesses.

This second choice clearly takes courage, but as the pages of this book will point out – history shows us that recessionary times are most often the best times to start and grow a wildly successful business.

One of the best things you can do as an entrepreneur or wantreprenenuer (someone *wanting* to start a business) is to hire an experienced business coach. For now, I encourage you to read this book and consider it a personal coaching session with me. As is my style and commitment, you'll find nothing but straight talk and honest opinions. If you offend easily or are a habitual 'doubting Thomas,' this may not be the book for you. However, if you have a good idea and a burning desire to start a business or you are running a business now and are tired of just getting by, but in either case can't muster the courage to pull the trigger, it is my sincere hope that this book will be like drinking a giant bottle of courage! If you turn the last page and say to yourself, "All right (your name here), time is a-wastin', let's get started right now," that result means two things will have happened.

One, this will be the best $20 you ever spent, and two, you will put a huge smile on my face – assuming you email, contact me online, post a comment on Facebook, or write a review on Amazon and share your joy! Either way, let's get started!

Acknowledgements

I'm writing this final section of my book in late August 2013, and I'm sitting at the edge of a small lake. The lake appears to be a sheet of glass. It is early morning, and this is time I discovered many years ago that I am most creative, so I no longer fight it. To me, this is the most perfect way to begin a day.

Stephanie and I are on vacation in the mountains of Massachusetts, and we've rented this fantastic cottage on this small lake. While there are many lake-front cottages we could have chosen, this one is close to where our daughters live and also the little guy who now lights up my world, my 'most amazing' grandson Nathan. So even though it's early and I'm on vacation, this seems like such a fitting place to finish this book and get it off to my editors.

As I have mentioned in my previous books, this is a special time of year for me for another important reason. It was twelve years ago that I was diagnosed with melanoma, and what a horribly frightening day that was. At one point the doctor explained to me that if my melanoma was stage III and not stage II (which it turned out to be), then the average survival rate at the time was 50-50 past five years.

So reaching the twelve-year mark as a cancer survivor is a big deal, and I am grateful beyond belief to God for helping me arrive at this milestone. I thank the Lord every day for blessing my life and business in truly unimaginable ways.

I want to thank my wife, Stephanie, for my being my best friend, constant companion, and biggest cheerleader for thirty-three years.

My four children, Nick, Steve, Jessica, and Amanda, have all moved on to their adult lives, and they continue to cheer me on, and I'm very proud of all of them. Since my last book both of my daughters have gotten married, and Jessica has blessed me with my first grandchild.

One of the greatest joys in my life has been helping Jessica start her home-based business, so she can be a stay-at-home mom to Nathan.

The amazing growth of my business would not be possible without my incredible support team. Thank you to my remarkable personal assistant and client service manager, Kate; my Sensei of my web presence, Adam; my lead designer, Chris; my interview scheduler and head of Pinterest marketing, Jessica;

Here's Grandpa Jim with Nathan moments after his birth.

amazing client support team members, Melanie and Lyndsay for providing outstanding client support to our hundreds of valued clients; Amy for her hundreds of 'Newsletter Guru' graphics; Julie-Ann, Sheridan and Matt for leading my team of content writers; Mike and his team from Mikel Mailings for printing and mailing my monthly No Hassle membership programs; Bobby, Jacki, and the entire team at Synapse for being outstanding partners in my Concierge Print and Mail On Demand program; and thank you to Ann Deiterich for doing a wonderful job editing this book (making me sound like a much better writer!).

A special thank you to Kevin Harrington for agreeing to write the foreword of this book. I'm a huge fan of the show Shark Tank on which Kevin appeared in the first two seasons. Kevin is truly an entrepreneur's entrepreneur and has been involved in over 500 product launches. He is the chairman of As Seen on TV, Inc.

Last but certainly not least, I want to thank the thousands of clients and subscribers whom we have the great pleasure of serving with our Smart Marketing and Business Building Programs, No Hassle Newsletters, No Hassle Social Media, Concierge Print and Mail on Demand, Success Advantage Publishing, No Hassle

Infographics, Customer Article Generator, my books, mastermind groups, newsletters, videos, podcasts, and my private coaching program. I can't remember when I've had more fun!

To Your Success,

Acknowledgements

Chapter One:
The Time is Right

The time is definitely right to build your dream business and start creating your own personal economic boom. Thinking about recent history, you may be scratching your head, wondering how I can make such a bold statement.

Case in point: The latter part of the first decade of the twenty-first century presented a bumpy ride for a lot of folks... bumpy at best. The stock market crash of September 2008 had most people sweating it out, worried about their investments, their retirement funds, or worse, worried about their very job security. In a single day at the end of that month, the Wall Street loss knocked out almost $1.2 trillion dollars in market value. Over a trillion. In one day. It was a roller coaster drop that no one enjoyed.

Too big to fail and government bailouts made headlines for weeks. Those were scary times and all too reminiscent of the stock market crash that led to the Great Depression. Were we headed toward that again? Was history bound to repeat itself? While we managed to evade a repeat of another full-blown depression, the Great Recession ensued, and everyone felt the pinch.

Since then, the economy has slowly recovered, very slowly, snail pace slowly. Slower than anyone would like. The unemployment rate still reflects an economy that doesn't have a solid foundation, and plenty of people are still underemployed. And guess what? That's good news! Especially if you find yourself among the ranks of the unemployed or underemployed.

Now you may think I'm really crazy making a statement like that, but I know this is a great time to launch and own a business. If you are unemployed or underemployed right now, trust me, I was once in your shoes, and deciding to launch my business was the best choice I ever made. Scary? You bet it was. But I did it, and so can you. That's the reason I decided to write this book: to help you understand that there's never been a better time to start a business.

Consider this: There are only so many corporate jobs at the top, just like there are only so many starting quarterback positions in the NFL. If you desire success, you are better off creating it yourself and carving out your own position at the top of your own enterprise.

Throughout these pages, I'll offer evidence and inspiration to help you decide to stop waiting for it to get easier. Here's a tip: No matter what

If you desire success, you are better off creating it for yourself than relying on anybody else.

you may be pursuing in your life, if you wait for it to get easier, you are going to wait forever. If you wait for it to get easier, you are never going to accomplish your goals. If you wait for it to get easier, time will pass you by, and years from now you'll probably be in exactly the spot you are now. So stop waiting for it to get easier! It's not going to.

Stuck in a Rut

Instead of being unemployed, perhaps you are defining yourself as underemployed. You have a job, and you tell yourself that you're grateful for it, especially whenever the unemployment figures are released. Chances are good you have friends, relatives, neighbors, or colleagues who faced joblessness in recent years. You've witnessed what they went through, and you want to avoid it at all costs. Job loss is a tough row to hoe, no matter how you slice it. In fact, depending on circumstances, it can be a devastating blow to your financial situation.

Clinging to your job, no matter how dead-end it may be, seems like a prudent choice, certainly better than the alternative, you tell yourself. You convince yourself that the benefits, dwindling as they may be, are worth sticking it out. Perhaps you work for a boss or with colleagues whom you don't respect. It fills eight hours every day with frustration, but again, you believe tolerating the frustration is a small price to pay to avoid unemployment. You try to convince yourself that pay day makes it worth sticking it out and putting up with it. You live for Fridays and find yourself dropping into a depressing funk on Sunday nights.

If you can relate to that scenario, you are definitely stuck in a rut, convincing yourself that the rut is better than facing unemployment. Running on the proverbial treadmill to guarantee a paycheck is better than the unknown. Guess what? Those aren't your only choices! Instead of running on the treadmill and trying (and maybe praying) to avoid unemployment, you can be your own boss, running your own business.

Never "trade hours for dollars." Your time and your life are far too precious!

When you choose to stay in the rut and on the treadmill, you are simply trading your hours for dollars, especially if you are in a job that neither uses your skill set nor challenges your creativity. Those hours you're trading are the precious ones that make up your life. Ask yourself honestly if it's worth it. Is it really worth it? Is putting up with underemployment in a job that's only tolerable at best worth your life? As the old saying goes, no one ever looked up from their death bed and proclaimed, "I wish I'd spent more time at the office in that dead end job!"

It's time to get out of the rut, off the treadmill, and start working for yourself and working for profits rather than working for a paycheck. It's an exciting and realistic alternative, and it is possible.

Personal Experience

As an entrepreneur, business building expert, and business coach, I've heard plenty of stories from others who made the choice to stop waiting for it to get easier and launch their businesses. None has regretted it. It's not always easy, and there's a lot to learn, but the consensus, like that of every entrepreneur, is that the work is always satisfying and rewarding.

In fact, I co-authored a book with Martin Howey, *It's Okay to Be Scared But Never Give Up*, in which we featured story after story of entrepreneurs who decided to stop waiting. One after the other shared the many challenges they faced in their businesses and their lives and what they did to overcome those obstacles. Some of the challenges, including the one both Martin and I faced, were life altering. You see, Martin and I are both cancer survivors.

Let me briefly share with you my story of becoming an entrepreneur and launching my own business. Through the years leading up to July 2000, I'd progressed and grew in my career, moving up the ranks from a retail store manager to a regional manager. Then I became part of a management team that franchised a small chain, growing from 14 stores to 80 stores and increasing our geographic footprint to 18 states. I took on creating the franchise training program and also handled the marketing for the company. Next stop, director of national franchise operations. After ten years, I was recruited to start a new marketing association for a chain of independently owned music stores. More success.

I'd done pretty well and was not feeling that I was in a rut or on a treadmill, but it all came to a screeching halt in July 2000 when I lost my job as vice president of marketing for a training company. The owner walked into my office and cut to the chase:

"We're eliminating your job. Your services are no longer needed." Wow. Just like that. If that wasn't bad enough, my job ended that very day. For the first time since I was 15 years old, I was without a job. Talk about scared!

I thought my unemployment would last for a few months, maybe, with me fielding and then deciding upon lucrative job offers. However, a few months turned into a year. I was doing everything I was supposed to do: networking, reading every newspaper, applying for jobs online, and being as creative about the whole process as I could be. This experience crushed my ego and self confidence.

Then one morning in the beginning of August in 2001, as I was trying to determine what I could do and how I could turn my situation around, I got a phone call. It was my doctor. Like my former employer, he cut to the chase: The diagnosis was cancer. My doctor insisted I needed to see a surgeon right away. I remember it being the first day of my wife's new full-time job. She was faced with telling her new boss that she couldn't come to work the next day, only her second day on the job, because she had to go with me to visit the surgeon.

The surgeon explained that he wouldn't know if it was stage II or stage III cancer until after the surgery. "Okay, so what's the difference?" I asked. He explained that with stage II, the average survival rate beyond five years is 80 percent. Without saying it out loud, I thought those odds sounded acceptable, even pretty good. Then he explained stage III: The average survival rate past five years is 50-50. Not at all good. My first thought was of my twin girls who were 13 years old at the time, and I became horribly frightened.

Thankfully, my skilled surgeon removed the melanoma, and it turned out to be stage II. It was a huge relief and an even bigger blessing. However, post surgery I was still unemployed and felt my life was terribly out of control. I often refer to this 15-month period as my personal 'season of crisis,' and frankly, it literally brought me to my knees. But this time, instead of simply praying to God for a job, I was on my knees praying for His wisdom and guidance. And that's when it became clear to me that I should put my skills and experience to work in launching my own business, and that's what I did in October 2001.

I haven't shared my story with you to make it sound like my situation was more devastating than the one you may be facing. Whatever your situation is, whether it's one of

I've been where you are now and can assure you, I've never looked back.

unemployment or underemployment or simply thinking that it might be time to get off the fence, I want to help you see that now is as good a time as any to scratch your entrepreneurial itch. It's never going to get easier and creating your own success, both professional and financial, can be achieved – if you get started now.

Stop Waiting and Get Going:

* It will never get easier; if you're waiting for it to get easier, you are going to wait forever.

* Although being underemployed brings the security of a paycheck, it brings little else. You are trading your precious hours for dollars. It's not really a fair trade-off. Your hours and your brain are more valuable.

* Those who have launched their own businesses have overwhelmingly shared stories of personal satisfaction and reward beyond a paycheck. You could join in that experience.

* This is an exciting and realistic time to launch a business.

Success Tips and Gems

Peter Drucker said, "The best way to predict the future is to create it." He's right. Get started today creating the future you want; nobody else is going to do it for you. And, if someone does try to tell you not to worry, they'll take care of everything for you, run away!

"Getting momentum going is the most difficult part of the job, and often taking the first step is enough to prompt you to make the best of your day." ~ Robert J. McKain

"Entrepreneurs and their small enterprises are responsible for almost all the economic growth in the United States." ~ Ronald Reagan. It's still true today!

"If things seem under control, you're just not going fast enough." I love this quote by Mario Andretti as it is rare to achieve significant growth and feel as though everything is going beautifully!

You can change or stay the same, keep doing what you've been doing or try something different, you can make the best of what you have or not, or you can smile or not – it's all your choice!

"If what you're working for really matters, you'll give it all you've got." Nido Qubein. I love this as the big lesson is that if you're not achieving your goals, perhaps they're not important enough!

Chapter Two:
Those Who Have Gone
Before

Let's be clear: I'm not simply using my coaching clients or my colleagues as examples to make my assertion that this is a great time to start a business. If that were the case, I wouldn't blame you for one second if you put this book down and asked for a refund!

In fact, there is example after example of entrepreneurs who started well-known businesses that became wildly successful during times of recession or worse, during the Great Depression. Although it may seem counterintuitive to launch a business during times of economic hardship, quite the opposite is true. Many businesses born out of this type of economic climate provided customers with better, faster, cheaper ways to do things, creating very successful entrepreneurs! And before you dimiss these examples as merely "successful businesses," remember this: every big business started small.

The founders of these businesses were sharp individuals who knew that they needed to fill a need or a niche in order to succeed. They studied the market and determined what customers wanted and needed, and then they figured out how to provide that. This is the foundation of business success. No matter what the economic climate may be and even in the very best of times, simply hanging out a shingle won't bring success. Hanging up the "open for business" sign will not cause people to beat a path to your door. Success comes from figuring out the need, figuring out the best way to fulfill it, and then doing that passionately and better than the competition.

I'd like to share a few examples of businesses that started during some of the worst economic times to help you understand that *now* is really a great time to launch a business.

The Great Depression and Before

After the Civil War, the railroad industry boomed. The country was expanding, and railroads became the nation's largest non-agricultural employer. Banks and other industries began heavily investing in railroads; however, when a firm heavily invested in railroad construction, Jay Cooke and Company, closed its doors in September 1873, many other firms followed suit, and the Panic of 1873 began. In the middle of that six-year recession, Thomas Edison opened his laboratory in Menlo Park, New Jersey, and the formation of General Electric followed a few years later. According to a recent Forbes study, GE is now the fourth largest company in the world.

Edison didn't focus on the economic climate. He focused on what he could do for people with the light bulb and, ultimately, all things electric. Moreover, in looking at GE today and its offerings, it has certainly expanded its realm, including healthcare innovations, aviation products, and imaging in addition to energy management, and oh yeah, light bulbs and appliances.

Even the Great Depression could not dampen true entrepreneurial spirit.
Let your dreams soar and make them reality.

The stock market crash of 1929 ushered in the Great Depression. Two Stanford University classmates, Bill Hewlett and Dave Packard, helped usher out that era in 1939 when they developed an electronic test instrument used by sound engineers in a garage in Palo Alto, California. Their first customer happened to be Walt

Disney. Despite starting with the meager investment of just over $500, Hewlett-Packard became the first technology business to exceed $100 billion in revenue.

Fortune magazine was founded in 1930, just four months after the Wall Street crash of 1929. In a memo to Time, Inc. written in November 1929, founder Henry Luce wrote, "We will not be over [sic] optimistic. We will recognize that this business slump may last as long as an entire year."

Although his assessment turned out to be overly optimistic indeed, or should I say "way overly optimistic," his magazine was selling for an unthinkable dollar per copy when the Sunday *New York Times* was only five cents. Luce was filling a need. Readers were willing to pay.

Cosmetics may have seemed like an overindulgence during the Great Depression, but Revlon began in 1932. Its first product was an opaque, long-lasting nail enamel that it sold to department stores and selected drugstores. There may not have been a need for the product, but there was a desire, and Revlon filled it. Revlon's revenue topped $1.4 billion at the end of 2012, having continued to increase and grow even throughout the Great Recession of the late 2000s.

The 1950s

The country saw two recessions during the 1950s, including the post-Korean War recession and the Eisenhower recession. Two notable companies got their starts during the first one, including Burger King and *Sports Illustrated*. The predecessor to what is now Burger King was founded in 1953 in Florida. The original founders were drawn to a piece of equipment known as an Insta-Broiler and saw potential in their innovative, assembly-line-style fast food production. Still known for its flame broiling, the Burger King® system now operates more than 12,200 restaurants in 76 countries around the world.

Sports Illustrated, as we know it today, began in 1954. Once again, it was a matter of filling a gap. Our friend, Henry Luce of *Time,* saw that there was no weekly sports magazine that covered actual events on a timely basis. Despite not being a sports fan and actually being advised against it, Luce decided the time was right and set out to create a magazine that was "not *a* sports magazine but *the* sports magazine." Today, it's estimated to be read by 23 million adults each week.

The Eisenhower recession of the late 1950s was the impetus for the founding of many well-known companies that are still in business today. Hyatt was founded by Jay Pritzker in 1957 when he purchased the Hyatt House motel, located adjacent to the Los Angeles International Airport. Now a global hospitality giant, Hyatt's worldwide portfolio consisted of nearly 500 properties, represented by nine different brands as of June 30, 2012.

Plenty of startups during tough times are still around today... and still enjoying success.

Moving from hotels to hotcakes, IHOP Corp. was another company that started during the Eisenhower recession. International House of Pancakes® opened its doors in 1958 in a Los Angeles suburb. They've seen over 1,500 restaurant openings across the country since that time.

Also founded in 1958 was Muppets, Inc. by puppeteer Jim Henson. The company started with *Sam and Friends,* a live-action puppet television show that was taped and aired locally in Washington, DC. One of the "friends" happened to be a lizard-like creature that evolved into Kermit the Frog. Henson tried for years to sell different shows to major American networks but was always unsuccessful. In 1976, he was approached by a British media mogul to produce a weekly show that became *The Muppet Show.*

Of course, the Muppets went on to be featured in several movies and became icons in and of themselves.

A chain of convenience stores known as Pronto Markets also got their start in 1958. You'll probably know this company by the name it took on in 1967: Trader Joe's. It now has over 350 stores across the country and is one of the hottest retailers around. Trader Joe's filled a need and a niche: It elevated food shopping from a chore to a cultural experience.

The 1970s

The Oil Crisis Recession lasted for 16 months in the early 70s. The unemployment rate at nearly nine percent was the third highest recorded during recessions or the Great Depression. Economic growth stagnated while oil prices soared. Within a year, gas rose a whopping fifty percent. Of course, with the high water mark for a gallon of gas reaching 55.1 cents in June 1974, it's hard to imagine that those prices caused economic woes. But they did, and cars lined up for blocks waiting to fuel up.

Rising fuel costs did not stop Frederick W. Smith from figuring out how to fill the need for businesses when "it absolutely, positively had to be there overnight." Federal Express began operations in 1973. Smith studied the country's transportation routes and saw that passenger routes were ineffective for moving packages and air freight. He had designs on becoming a government contractor but didn't get the contract. However, on April 17 of that year, 14 small aircraft departed from Memphis International Airport, and Federal Express delivered 186 packages to 25 US cities from Rochester, NY to Miami. The company saw a need and figured out how to fill it. Today it's estimated that FedEx ships 1.2 billion packages annually.

One company that did start as a government contractor that same year was LexisNexis, the document and information retrieval company. It introduced a legal-research system that dramatically changed the way legal research and analyses were conducted, ushering the legal profession into a new era. Today, it serves legal, corporate, government, and academic markets in 100 countries on six continents, providing the most authoritative sources in the world.

LexisNexis may not be a household name, but Microsoft is. In 1975, Bill Gates dropped out of Havard and started this little company that dealt with computing languages. If you're using a PC or any of its popular software programs, Microsoft touches much of what you accomplish in a day. Gates saw the benefit of what a disk operating system could do, and cornered the market. 'Nuff said. You know the rest of that story.

Recession-based Media Startups

The early 80s saw another series of recessions, again driven by energy crises. The Iran/Energy Crisis Recession saw unemployment rates second only to those that occurred during the Great Depression. A network was launched on June 1, 1980 with this introduction:

Technology paves the way for innovations and out-of-the-box thinking.

"We won't be signing off until the world ends. We'll be on, we'll be covering it live, and that will be our last, last event. We'll play the national anthem for one time on the first of June, and that's all. When the end of the world comes, we'll play 'Nearer My God to Thee' before we sign off." The speaker was Ted Turner. The station was The Cable News Network. Was there a need for 24-hours news? The success of CNN proved there was, and it changed the way we anticipate receiving news – immediately. There was no longer a need to wait for Walter Cronkite at 6:30 p.m.

A little over a year later, another station was introduced with these words: "Ladies and gentlemen, rock and roll." MTV aired its first music video, appropriately, "Video Killed the Radio Star" by the Buggles on August 1, 1981 and introduced a whole new way of consuming music. Musicians were now making visual recordings in addition to audio ones. Video jockeys, or VJs, played the same role as their radio counterparts: filling the transition between videos.

Music videos took on a life of their own, and money was invested in making creative, often cutting-edge videos. Fans were as likely to get their music from their televisions as they were from their radios. Success came with a new use of technology.

Another media giant grew dramatically during the Post-9/11 recession. No matter how much stock you may place on it or whether you love it or loathe it, Wikipedia started in January 2001. By the end of its first year, it contained 20,000 articles in 18 languages. It crossed the million mark in 2006. As a contributor-based site, many people have taken it with a grain of salt, but a 2005 study by *Nature* found its science entries to be nearly as accurate as *Britannica*. Founders tapped into the public's desire to share the information they had.

Clearly, there is no shortage of examples that prove that the economic climate should never be the litmus test for the right time to start a business. You may be surprised to learn that many of the behemoth businesses of today got their starts during the worst of times. Their founders determined the need and pursued it passionately. Think any of Bill Gates' classmates at Harvard thought he would one day stand at the helm of a computer giant? Doubtful. Henry Luce launched two successes in the face of his naysayers. And Ted Turner had the chutzpah to insist his station would never go off the air… and to this point, it hasn't.

The right time to launch your business is right now.

Stop Waiting and Get Going:

❖ It may seem counterintuitive to start your business in the face of a tough economy, but that's probably the exact right time to do so. When you can fill a need or desire for customers who are probably facing the same economic hardships, you have the foundation of success.

❖ Think about your passions and skills. Then study the market to determine where those intersect with a need or desire for a niche.

❖ Ignore the economy. It has no bearing on business success.

 Success Tips and Gems

In order to succeed, you must first be willing to fail. Do not worry about missteps, errors, or failing. It only means that you are taking action and moving forward.

"Successful people are always looking for opportunities to help others. Unsuccessful people are asking, 'What's in it for me?'" ~ Brian Tracy

"My biggest motivation is to just to keep challenging myself. I see life almost like one long University education that I never had – everyday I'm learning something new" ~ Richard Branson

If you succeed big time your first time at bat, try not to look surprised as you run the bases!

"Greatness is not a function of circumstance. Greatness is largely a matter of conscious choice and discipline." ~ Jim Collins

Don't "pre-judge" outcomes when trying something different. Failing to try something because you somehow "know" in advance it won't work will likely cost you some great opportunities. Once in a while, you have to just take the shot!

Wealth rewards risk and speed. Playing it 'safe' may be the safe thing to do, but successful entrepreneurs are risk takers. You have to take the shot. Wealth is also attracted to speed. Learn to get things done fast, become an implementation machine!

Always be hungry! Successful entrepreneurs have a constant hunger for more knowledge to improve themselves, their marketing, and their program offerings.

"Don't judge each day by the harvest you reap but by the seeds you plant." ~ Robert Louis Stevenson (The businesses that experience regular and predictable growth are generally those that are always planting seeds!)

Those Who Have Gone Before

Chapter Three:
There's No Time Like the Present

So, will you be the next Bill Gates, Henry Luce, or Ted Turner? It's certainly not impossible, and of course, you won't know until you try, and now is certainly a great time to do just that.

As I've stated and based on examples in the previous chapter, a poor economic climate should never stop anyone from deciding to start a business. In fact, in this chapter we'll explore why starting a business in a recession makes all the sense in the world.

Being a successful entrepreneur is not about having a huge idea; it's about filling a need, solving a problem, and providing value. Your enterprise can certainly grow into something huge, but you don't need a killer idea to start. Most businesses have morphed and evolved from where they started. The willingness to morph and evolve, always looking for ways to grow once you've launched is the sign of a true entrepreneur.

You may have colleagues or even family members who will question your decision to launch your business now; however, keep in mind that recessions are typically followed by periods of extraordinary growth. Since World War II, most of the recessions we've faced have lasted an average of ten months and those periods were followed by growth cycles that lasted an average of 50 months. While the most recent Great Recession exceeded the ten-month average, no one has a crystal ball that can predict how long the next growth cycle will last. Indicators are good that the worst part of the Great Recession is probably behind us. Employment statistics, the stock market, and the housing market are trending favorably.

Making the move and launching your business now is like investing in the stock market: you want to jump in and buy when stocks are low and starting to rise. You want to jump in and start your business before the next growth cycle really gets rolling. Here are several reasons to stop waiting and get serious about launching your business.

Prices

To start, prices are low – all prices. The investments you need to make in launching your business will probably not be cheaper than they are now. Startup costs are lower than ever. This includes low prices and great deals in all categories, including office space, equipment,

A good thing about a bad economy: Low prices across the board.

technology, supplies, inventory, real estate, and personnel. You'll find that whatever investments you need to make in order to get your business off the ground will not be lower until the end of the growth cycle we're probably about to enter and the start of the next recession.

Talking about the next recession while encouraging you to launch your business now may seem very pessimistic; however, history indicates that there will be another one. History also indicates that based on the length of the Great Recession that's slowly coming to a close, the growth cycle we're likely to enter will also exceed the average four-plus-year length of previous growth cycles. One of the most prosperous economies the country ever experienced occurred after the Great Depression.

Do you really want to wait four years or possibly longer to create your own economic boom, continuing to work for a paycheck week after week rather than working for yourself and for profits right now?

Technology

Technology advancements have opened new ways of conducting business and new opportunities in and of themselves. The growing use of tablets and smartphones mean you can do business from anywhere there's Internet connectivity. Technology has leveled the playing field. Even a single-person operation can easily look big. Creating your own website without programming skills is now possible.

The digital revolution brought with it a whole new industry – Information Technology consulting, support and repair. It's a boon to those with the needed skill sets. Let's face it, we all use technology, but how many of us truly know what's going on behind the scenes or how to fix "all things digital" when they go awry... as they invariably will.

People

While prices are low, the talent pool is high. The recession brought countless layoffs. Talented professionals were let go for no other reason than cutbacks and company belt-tightening. These folks are now not only in the job market, they may also be very leery about jumping back into the corporate world and eager to join an enterprise at the ground floor.

Technology has also made finding employees easier than ever. Social media has increased our networking opportunities exponentially. No doubt you know someone who knows someone who would be perfect for your company. Depending on the type of business you plan to launch, your employees could all be virtual. It's not unthinkable that you could hire or contract someone from across the country or around the globe.

New Suppliers

Most companies have scrutinized every penny they spent and cost incurred over the last several years. We were all looking for ways to save money. Even long-standing vendor relationships were put under the microscope. It opened the door to change.

As a potential new supplier, you may have the advantage. Even if you are not the least expensive, buyers may find your product or service with the fresh approach you bring very attractive. It circles back to the basic concept of filling a need or a niche and doing it better and with more passion than your competitors.

Tax Advantages

You can gain tax advantages as a business owner that are not available to you as an employee. I'll be the first to admit that gaining a tax advantage is no single reason to start a business; however, it adds to the benefit of being an entrepreneur.

For example, if you operate your business out of your home, you will be able to deduct portions of household expenses (utilities, insurance, etc.) as part of your business expenses and lower your tax liability. Additionally, depending on how your business is structured, you may be able to take certain expenses as deductions that you can't otherwise, including the ability to deduct medical expenses beyond what you can write off on Schedule A. And that's really only the tip of the iceberg.

Investment Opportunity

The stock market crash of 2008 made all but the most diehard investors a little bit jittery and nervous to continue buying stocks and investing in the market. Slumping interest rates that are really showing no indication of improving anytime soon make secure investments like CDs or traditional savings accounts very unattractive.

That said, you may find that family and friends are more amenable to investing in your company and financing a portion of your start up and/or operating costs. Of course you'll need a solid business plan that shows your ability to deliver results.

Another option is to consider a web-based capital raising campaign. There are quite a few players to consider in this arena like Kickstarter.com, indiegogo.com, StartSomeGood.com, crowdfunder.com, and Rockethub.com, just to name a few. Do a little homework to find out which one might work best for you and your venture. There are pros and cons to each and to the idea of crowdfunding itself. It may give you access to needed capital and establish a customer base, but it may also be "all or nothing" and is not suited for every venture. There are both success and failure stories in this arena. Please do your due diligence.

Credit

In addition to finding low prices, you'll probably find that vendors are willing to extend credit to continue growing their own companies. They need to survive like everybody else, and gaining you as a new customer can provide a win-win situation. Again, a well-thought out idea and business plan are must haves in order to take advantage.

Exposure

Technology and circumstances combine favorably for someone launching a business. You are no longer limited by the publicity you can get from your local newspaper or media outlet. The sky's the limit when it comes to announcing your business opening. You can use social media to begin gaining traction and building buzz immediately.

There is an insatiable need for content, especially fresh content. You can blog in your area of expertise, provide guest blogging for complementary sites, and offer to be interviewed about your product, service, or business venture. Although you don't have to rely on your local newspaper for coverage, you'll probably find that there's interest in your story: your new business shows local economic growth. Don't hesitate to shout about it!

Even Better Prices

I've already mentioned that prices are low and that you can probably find most of what you need at very attractive pricing. You may find even better pricing by purchasing at auction. There is no shortage of auctions, and you can typically find everything from desks and furniture to vehicles and heavy equipment. Be open to doing a bit of searching and homework, and by buying used, you can easily come out ahead.

Take Over

Speaking of doing your homework, you may want to consider taking over another business. There are plenty of businesses that are launched by people who don't have the right skill set or the passion to make the business profitable. These people may have started when times were good or had more money than business sense or willingness to learn. Now they want to exit at any cost.

You may be able to find a great deal simply by taking over the lease, and you can create a win-win situation: The previous owner can exit (and potentially minimize losses) and you get the opportunity to turn around a business, make it successful, and create your own economic boom.

What Else Are You Going To Do?

If you lost your job and your unemployment has extended for longer than you anticipated (as was my case!), you have to do something. The need for income and to be productive is a driving force. Settling for underemployment may seem like the safer route, but it's truly a dead end. You will stagnate quickly and may find yourself right back where you are today with nothing to show for it but lost time.

There's no shame in needing income, and that need may be the impetus you need not only to start a business but to make it succeed and be profitable quickly. And there's certainly nothing wrong with that approach!

Choose to pave your own way. Never choose the dead end!

While your age (if you're a Baby Boomer) may work against you in landing a new job, there is no age discrimination in entrepreneurship. In fact, according to a Kauffman Foundation study (one of the largest foundations dedicated to entrepreneurship), Baby Boomers now represent 23 percent of new entrepreneurs, nearly ten percent higher than in 1996. The 20-something wunderkinds like Mark Zuckerberg or YouTube founders, Chad Hurley, Steve Chen and Jawed Karim, are the exceptions.

Just as there was no shortage of examples of businesses that started during the worst of economic times and became profitable creating economic booms for their founders, there is no shortage of reasons not to start a business. We just covered more than ten very good ones.

A growth cycle, and potentially a very large one, could be right around the corner. That's both good news and bad news. The good news is that we can all benefit from better economic times. The bad news is that the clock is running, and the longer you wait to start your enterprise, the less chance you may have to fully capitalize on an improved economy. Remember the analogy to investing in the stock market? As stock prices start to rise, the sooner you should jump in. The same is true for launching your business.

Stop Waiting and Get Going:

❖ Prices are low, but they won't stay low. Getting started will never be cheaper. Plus, you can find great deals at auctions.

❖ The labor pool is high, and innovative technologies provide the opportunity for virtual work (if it applies to your enterprise) or at least great ways to find great employees.

❖ Existing companies are more amenable to finding new suppliers, and creating better, faster, cheaper ways to fill the need gives you the advantage.

❖ Your business can provide tax advantages to you, and potential investment opportunities for your friends and family.

❖ Publicity is easier to attain, thanks to the Internet, than it ever has been.

❖ There's no age discrimination in entrepreneurship.

❖ You have to do something, so why not work for yourself and your own profitability?

 Success Tips and Gems

You don't need 100 new ideas. Take two or three good ideas, add a healthy dose of urgency, sprinkle in some massive action, and then top off with some intense focus!

Growing a business during a difficult economy is not for the timid. It requires bold, decisive, and relentless action. Success today requires a higher level of intensity, focus, determination, and a healthy dose of daily urgency. Make it happen!

The Secret to a Successful Business (It's almost embarrassingly simple): Provide outstanding value combined with world-class service and you'll have higher profits and more customers for life!

Stop making things more complicated than they need to be. Just get started and enjoy the inevitable twists and turns in the road!

Great ideas are fun, but it's the relentless effort of action and implementation that gets you to the finish line. Remember, to finish strong you have to first get started!

"Even if you're on the right track, you'll get run over if you just sit there." ~ Will Rogers (I love this quote, makes me think about taking action!)

Focus your time on high-revenue generating tasks. If you think you're saving money by doing it all yourself and refusing to hire experts or assistants, you're wrong. You're paying with your time, and that's far more valuable than an assistant's invoice.

Procrastination is the grave in which opportunity is buried.

There's No Time Like the Present

Chapter Four:
Types of Business

So you're thinking of starting out on your own. You want to create your dream business and work for profits rather than trading hours for dollars but may be unsure of what business to pursue. Or possibly, you're not clear on the best way to bring your idea to the marketplace.

I'm not writing this book to be a Business Startup Bible with all the information you may need to consider regarding the type of business to launch or the best business structure to create (e.g. sole proprietorship, partnership, LLC, or corporation). My goal is to get you off the dime and understand that it is possible to create your own economic boom by launching a business.

That said, I do want to take a few pages to review different types of businesses to consider that may help solidify your idea and help you see that you probably already have some of the building blocks in place as a result of all of your previous work and career experience. Each one has its pros and cons.

Franchises

There is no shortage of franchise opportunities available. They result from someone who had a great idea, pursued it, and then grew it in order to sell the idea and foundation to someone else, possibly someone like you. That's exactly what happened with the bike store business I ran many years ago.

The primary benefit of operating a franchise is name recognition to start along with national marketing that benefits your operation. Additionally, you will find that policies and procedures as well as marketing materials are already carved out, so you don't need to start from scratch with any of those. Plus there are so many opportunities that you can pick and choose one that fits your interests and suits your lifestyle from restaurants to cleaning services and everything in between.

While many franchisors will offer financing, there may be a hefty fee to get started, and you may be held accountable to sales quotas and required to solely purchase equipment and supplies from the home office.

E-Commerce

Like I said earlier, technology has leveled the playing field and e-commerce has opened a wealth of retail and retail-like opportunities. Anyone with Internet connectivity can create a website and begin selling from anywhere, even your own home. Fear of purchasing online has long evaporated, and many consumers prefer the ease and convenience of online shopping. If you're not convinced of that, review Amazon's growth and latest annual report. You can be up and running quickly, often with minimal startup costs. In some cases, you never even have to stock inventory, or you can start an information publishing business.

An e-commerce business might just be the easiest one to start, and that's actually a double-edged sword. Because it's easy, there is a lot of competition. Finding the right target audience and driving traffic to your site is not easy. If you are selling hard products (possibly even something you create), there are associated warehousing and shipping logistics you'll have to contend with.

Consulting and Freelancing

Starting a consulting or freelancing business lets you put your years of experience and expertise to work for you in order to gain profits. You can continue to focus on your niche and pick and choose the clients with whom you want to work. There are many people who enjoy working on a contract or project basis, and this is an area that is growing exponentially.

More people are opting for contract-based work, working from home and according to their own schedules, than ever. Once again, technology has made this increasingly possible. You can easily be a virtual "employee," working on one project until completion and then starting the next one or even juggling many projects at once.

The recent economic downturn forced companies to cut staff and are now more open than ever before to using virtual employees. Additionally, with a probable growth cycle on the horizon, many companies are turning to consultants to find better, faster, cheaper ways of doing business and improving their processes and procedures.

The downside of this type of business is simply summed up: You eat what you kill. You're responsible for your own sales and marketing with no guarantee of steady income. That may seem scary, but remember what I said at the beginning about being stuck in a rut. If you are trading hours for dollars, clinging to a steady paycheck and benefits, and working in a job you hate, you are wasting your life. Is it really worth it?

Pick the business type that best suits your idea, your situation, and your passion.

Direct Selling/Network Marketing

Like franchises, there are plenty of opportunities in this arena along with the opportunity to make very good money. It's hard to imagine the Avon Lady making six figures, but it's certainly possible with persistence and dedication – the foundation of any successful business.

From cosmetics to jewelry to vitamins to financial products... well, just about everything and anything is available via the direct selling platform. There are low startup costs and flexible hours. Most models let you work your way up, providing residual income from the efforts for those who you subsequently recruit.

You do need sales skills to succeed, and any good sales person will also tell you that you need a thick skin since rejection is all part of the process. But with self-confidence and optimism, the sky's the limit.

Stop Waiting and Get Going:

❖ If you are uncertain about what you want to do or how to bring your idea to market, there are various types of businesses to get you started.

❖ No matter which one you may choose to pursue, there are pros and cons to each.

❖ In every case, income isn't guaranteed, but you are free to pursue what you want, and with persistence and dedication, you can create your dream business and your own economic boom.

 Success Tips and Gems

Operate Your Business with a Sense of Urgency. Thought #1: Take all your goals and cut the due dates in half (at least)! That is, don't start writing your book next month, start it tomorrow!

Operate Your Business with a Sense of Urgency. Thought #2: Bring your well thought out program to market sooner rather than later and course correct as you go!

In reality, the reason more of your customers or prospects don't buy from you is that you haven't done enough to build your customers' trust in your products or services. Do a better job of your building trust and you'll close more sales!

The speed and height to which you will grow your business is often revealed not only in your daily routine but also in the energy and enthusiasm that you bring to each day.

Be patient with marketing. Results are seldom immediate and the full benefit (potential profit) of any campaign may be measured over months or years (lifetime customer value). People buy when they're ready to buy, and your job is to remain top-of-mind, so you're the first one they think of when they're ready.

'Myth' Buster: Your product is so great it will sell itself. False! Even after establishing that there is a need, nothing gets sold until the people with the need become aware of your solution. Translation: Aggressive targeted marketing.

The minute a customer starts to ask, "Can you...?," your mind should be focused on thinking about "How can I...?" And if possible, try to provide the extra "something" for free. The extra "wow" you create will likely be infinitely more valuable than the extra expense.

Entrepreneurial Freedom:
- *Want to own an 'in demand' product/service? Create one.*
- *Want to have a stellar reputation? Earn one.*
- *Want to have a best-selling book? Write one.*
- *Want a big responsive list? Be a 'giver' and grow one.*
- *Want others to promote your business? Promote theirs first.*
- *Want more referrals? Create raving fans daily.*
- *Want to own a profitable business? Build one.*

Chapter Five:
The True and Real Nature
of a Successful Business

This may be the most important chapter in this book as it deals with your mindset. To create a successful and profitable business, certain skill sets are needed, but a proper mindset is essential. Let's talk about profit.

My ears perked up on a recent trip when I overheard a conversation at the airport about "businesses that profit from other people's pain." The person I overheard speaking clearly had a very negative view of entrepreneurship. Or possibly he had a very negative view of any business turning a profit. I wasn't sure if he was differentiating the two, but it got me thinking while I spent the next three and a half hours in a silver tube flying to my destination.

I'll be the first to admit that there is no shortage of stories about unscrupulous CEOs who are profiteering crooks. Very simply, if they broke the law, they should be in jail. The likes of Bernie Madoff or Jeff Skilling (former CEO of Enron) get no sympathy from me, and as far as I'm concerned, should not get sympathy from anyone. They illegally profited and caused a lot of people a lot of pain. Both of them (along with a laundry list of other CEOs who committed white-collar crimes and were caught) are serving the jail sentences they deserve.

Dealing with Catastrophes

My problem and slight irritation with the "greedy SOB" point of view and mentality that I overheard is that somehow any business owner who makes a profit from other people's misery or pain should simply find another line of work. What strikes me as odd is that, at its core, entrepreneurship is the ability to profit by solving problems for others... or in effect, curing their pain!

You may not equate solving problems with curing pain, but I assure you they are one and the same. Now the guy I overheard in the airport was possibly referring to businesses that profit from their customers who may be dealing with a catastrophe. However, even those types of businesses must be profitable in order to continue serving other customers... to continue easing their pain. And where would we be without those businesses when we needed them?

Look at a company like SERVPRO® – the fire and water damage restoration service. If it wouldn't be for catastrophes like fires and floods, this company would not be in business. None of

Integrity and profitability are not mutually exclusive. You can ease pain and earn profit.

us wants to think about that sort of catastrophe hitting our homes or businesses, but the reality is that fires and floods do happen. If a company like SERVPRO® didn't turn a profit, they'd close up shop and wouldn't be there to serve the next customer who needed them. And if a company like that were not in business, who would you turn to after a catastrophe when you were suffering the pain of property loss and needed a cleaning and restoration service?

There are also pro-active examples: alarm companies. If there were no break-ins or burglaries, there would be no need for alarm companies. If you've ever been the victim of this type of crime, you know how very unsettling the experience is even if nothing of value were stolen or vandalized. These security companies provide a certain level of peace of mind and may help prevent a break-in in the first place. Peace of mind eases pain.

If rocks or the occasional thug didn't smash car windows, there'd be no need for window repair companies. If bugs and other vermin didn't invade your home, there'd be no need for exterminators or pest control. There is no shortage of examples like this, and aren't you glad these companies are there when *you* need them? Are they profiting from your pain? In a sense, yes; however, they aren't causing you pain... they're easing it. They're solving a problem you may have, be it a cracked or smashed windshield or termites.

Providing Solutions

No doubt you have skill that can solve someone else's problem, and that's the very heart of the business you're about to launch or may have already launched. You have an opportunity to solve a problem or ease a pain and in the process, create wealth for yourself by being profitable.

If you're skilled at getting clients and some business owner desperately needs clients, you can solve his problem and ease his pain. Depending on his situation, it may even border on being catastrophic: He could lose his business without an influx of new clients, and his business supports twenty employees who would then be out of work. Is this a catastrophe on par with someone losing their house to fire or valuables to burglary? Just ask any of the twenty employees who may be facing a lay off.

Or maybe you're skilled at designing and creating cool websites. I am certain there are countless business owners floundering and in frustration and pain because they don't have the first darn clue how to do it. Their business success depends on their online presence, so yeah, they're in pain. If you can solve that pain, don't you deserve to turn a profit, so you can stay in business and help other entrepreneurs with their websites? Don't you deserve to put your expertise to work and build wealth because of it?

It reminds me of the story of the home heating repairman who was called in to fix a furnace. There was no heat in the house, and the temperatures were well below freezing. The lack of heat was a pain, if not a catastrophe, for the homeowner. The repair man came in, surveyed the situation, turned one screw, and handed the homeowner an invoice for $200. "$200?" the homeowner cried when he looked at the invoice. "But you only turned one screw!" With that, the repairman took back the invoice, adjusted it, and handed it back to the homeowner. Now it read: "Turning one screw: $1.00; knowing which screw to turn to provide a warm house: $199.00."

The very foundation of entrepreneurial success is putting your skill and expertise to work to solve someone else's pain and turn a profit by doing so. That pain may be generally accepted as truly catastrophic as in the example of a house that burns down, or it may only be considered catastrophic by the person who is dealing with the pain, like the business owner doesn't know how to build a website. Regardless, business success depends on solving a problem, not matter how big or small others deem that problem to be.

In my opinion, too many people struggle with the view that business owners are being opportunistic and simply profiting from other people's problems. As long as you play by the rules, don't cheat, operate your business with integrity, and pay your taxes, then by all means step up to the plate, launch your business, and solve other people's problems and cure their pain... and work to create a nice tidy profit for yourself.

Stop Waiting and Get Going:

❖ Profitability and integrity are not mutually exclusive, but any entrepreneur who cheats or breaks the law deserves to go to jail.

❖ No one should have a negative view of businesses that step in when catastrophes strike and earn a profit by the service they provide. That profit means they'll still be in business to help you or the next person who needs them.

❖ There's nothing wrong with putting your skill and expertise to work to earn what you're worth.

❖ The foundation of business is solving a problem and curing pain, no matter how catastrophic or small anyone else views that pain to be.

 Success Tips and Gems

Your skill and talent, combined with the way you deliver it, is what makes you truly unique. Beware that you don't fall into the trap of thinking that what you do is common, simply because others do it, or because you've been doing it for a long time. If you provide value – charge appropriately!

"Successful people usually don't talk about profitability or success. They usually focus on providing greater value and purpose." ~ Frank Luntz

Don't take your skills for granted. They may seem commonplace to you because you've been doing it for so long. View the value of what you offer from your customers' perspectives.

Work smarter, not harder is a popular phrase. But if you're not charging what you're worth, based on the value you're providing, chances are you're working much harder than you need to be!

Forget how long it takes you. Evaluate the product or service you provide based on the end result benefit and what pain it cures, or what joy it brings to your customer, and then set your pricing based on that!

I've never met a highly successful entrepreneur who wasn't passionate about their program and the solutions they offer. Because without passion it would be impossible to work the occasional 16-hour days or endure the challenges every business owner faces!

Chapter Six: Entrepreneur vs. Small Biz Owner

Whenever I write, speak, or record videos, you'll often hear me say "entrepreneurs and small business owners," and occasionally someone will ask me what the difference is. I think in many ways, it is mindset. Here are my thoughts.

A small business person is typically someone who owns a business, whether it's a brick and mortar store front or even a home-based business. It is certainly possible for an entrepreneur to own a small business. So Jim, where's the difference?!

As I said, it is largely mindset. Small business owners usually think about growing their businesses by simply selling more of whatever they sell. If they run a carpet store, they want to sell as much carpet as they can out of their location, and when that is maxed out, they look for another location to open as the way to continue selling more carpet. Another example: Let's say you run a home-based business where you offer a pool cleaning service or perhaps a residential home cleaning service. Such a small business owner is usually focused on cleaning as many pools or homes as they can, and when they feel they've maxed out their ability to grow, they'll add staff and/or look to get hired in other territories.

The flip side of this thinking is what I like to describe as an agile, fast-moving entrepreneur. Instead of being single minded and desiring to sell as much of their core product or service as they can, entrepreneurs are focused on wealth creation. In other words, they are open to and desire multiple streams of revenue and are also open to exploring new ideas and services to offer current clients or new clients. Instead of singularly focusing on driving more sales, they're looking for ways to create wealth.

Let's use my business experience as an example. When I started my first business in October 2001, it was called Dynamic Communication, and my sole focus was writing and designing newsletters for corporations, Chambers of Commerce, associations, and nonprofits. Four years later, I had 25 clients and was making a nice living. I began to wonder how many more clients I could add as I was running out of time in the day, and I was determined at the time not to have employees.

I thought life was good until my wife, Stephanie, asked me a question one night after dinner. It was an innocent question but one that actually rocked my world! She asked me, "Jim, when are we going to go on vacation?" You see, it had been at least five years since we'd had a vacation, but when she asked me that question; my first thought was not, "How can we afford it?" Instead, my first thought was, "I can't go away; there's nobody to run my business!"

I realized at that very moment that I didn't create a business; I had created a job. I made a decision several days later to spend the next six to twelve months starting over, and instead of being a small business owner, I wanted to be an entrepreneur.

My first step was to figure out how to use leverage. How could I leverage my skill and talent writing and designing newsletters, but get paid by multiple clients instead of one at a time? And so, in 2006 I launched my second business, No Hassle

Make sure you create a business, not a job. Keeping thinking about growth opportunities!

Newsletters! Today I serve hundreds of clients in nine countries with my famous 'Customer Loving Content^TM' and ready-to-go newsletter templates.

Next, I was on the hunt for more and different ways to generate sales and create wealth, and the answers came from my own customers! After launching No Hassle Newsletters, I launched The Newsletter Guru's Concierge Print and Mail on Demand Program, and I now print thousands of newsletters for clients all over the country.

Step three was to add my Custom Article Generator, which is a program where I offer the skill and talent of my writers to write custom articles for my customers. This service keeps my writers busy, and since creating content is a never ending struggle, my customers love the service.

In March of 2011, I created and launched another popular marketing program, No Hassle Social Media. No Hassle Social Media is an amazing content program for entrepreneurs and small business owners who need a ton of content, articles, blog posts, and more, so they can keep feeding their 'content is king' social media marketing machine.

I then launched No Hassle InfoGraphics Generator to offer custom 'Pinterest' style infographics to entrepreneurs who see the value in harnessing the amazing web traffic that Pinterest is currently creating.

I created Success Advantage Publishing to print my books and several information marketing products, and we're also starting to publish some books for my private coaching clients!

Finally, at least for now, I am in my fifth year coaching entrepreneurs and small business owners internationally on how to market and grow a more profitable business faster. I run an international mastermind group and offer private coaching to a limited number of entrepreneurs. You can learn more about these services by visiting www.TheNewsletterGuru.com.

The lesson I hope you learn from my example (other than I am very busy) is that one, it is never too late to start a business; and two, it is never too late to recreate an existing business to become one of multiple revenue streams that do more to create wealth than it would to simply focus on selling more of your goods or services through your current business.

Stop Waiting and Get Going:

❖ The difference between a small business owner and an entrepreneur (in my opinion) is only a matter of mindset.

❖ Small business owners, whether they operate brick-and-mortar locations, online businesses, or provide a service see growth only through the lens of selling more of their core product or service.

❖ There's nothing wrong with being a small business owner. Just be careful that you are truly launching a business and not simply "creating a job."

❖ Entrepreneurs look for multiple revenue streams and other products and services that complement their core offering as a way of not simply growing their business but building wealth as well.

❖ It's never too late to re-direct an existing business to grow in several directions rather than by relying on increasing sales.

 Success Tips and Gems

"Most people spend 90% of their time on what they're not best at, and only 10% of their time on their best ability. Successful people delegate that 90% and are thus able to spend all their time on their "unique" ability." ~ Gary Halbert (Entrepreneurs, this is perhaps

the most powerful thing you will read. It will mean even more if you adapt it in your business.)

"The entrepreneur in us sees opportunities everywhere we look, but many people see only problems everywhere they look. The entrepreneur in us is more concerned with discriminating between opportunities than he or she is with failing to see the opportunities."~ Michael Gerber

Successful entrepreneurs are prepared to take risks and step outside their comfort zone to get what they want. Real growth often comes from a place of discomfort. Think about it!

Legendary businessman, Harvey McKay, wrote a book titled "Dig Your Well Before You're Thirsty." The title contains a powerful lesson for all entrepreneurs. Do at least one thing every day (I call it planting seeds) to increase your chances of attracting more business.

Entrepreneurs replace the word "fail" with "test." It's less scary and only through much "testing" will you find out what really works!

Chapter Seven: Business GPS

GPS, or the Global Positioning System, is the satellite navigation system so many of us have grown to depend on to get us to practically any place on planet Earth. Whether you are picturing yourself as an entrepreneur or small business owner, there is another GPS system that I would like to introduce you to.

I've come to realize that this GPS system is the one that makes some entrepreneurs or small business owners more successful than others. It is the system that some entrepreneurs use to turn any challenge or difficult situation into a home run. I know a lot of people who have increased their "batting average" by using this system. On the other hand, I've met and coached some entrepreneurs and small business owners who either struggle to make the right decisions or can't seem to take the leap to move their businesses forward.

The economy, whether it's good or bad, is a level playing field for all business owners. When it's good, it's good for everyone, and when the economy is sluggish or even downright poor, it's that way for everyone as well. The GPS system I'm about to introduce you to is the game changer.

This GPS system stands for Guts, Persistence, and Strategy.

Guts

When it comes to guts, there are actually two parts of it. First is "guts" as in courage and the ability to make and execute hard decisions. The second part of it is learning to trust your gut, your intuition.

Business owners face tough decisions and hard choices every day. Without a doubt, it takes guts to run a business, and there are three stages of guts, or courage, in the life of any entrepreneur.

The first stage is simply having the guts to pull the trigger. There are millions of people who dream about starting a business. They have an idea for a new or improved product or service that they're convinced will help others; however, few of them actually have the guts to pull the trigger and start their businesses. There could be several reasons for this, including a lack of startup funds, fear of failure, or, believe it or not, fear of success. The bottom line is that starting a business takes guts – a lot of guts.

Entrepreneurship takes two kinds of guts: Guts to launch and then courage to always trust your gut.

I remember when I started my business in the fall of 2001. I was full of excitement and enthusiasm, I spent weeks making decisions, planning, designing a logo (admittedly important but not the most important thing I could have been doing at the time!), and filling out paperwork and new business applications. Then I got to my first roadblock.

I was filling out an application to start a new business, and it required a $50 fee. Certainly this was not a lot of money (except that I was broke at the time), but up until this point, all of my actions had not required an investment. Suddenly I was faced with the need to spend money on my dream of starting a business, and it suddenly made it very real and very public. I was scared because this investment represented the feeling of "no turning back now."

After 15 months of unemployment, spending money needlessly was certainly not an option. Therefore, spending money on my dream – even a paltry $50 – took guts. I actually had to become a businessman and start doing the hard work. Yikes!

The second stage, when a whole lot more in the way of guts is required, is during the lean startup years. I'll admit that my first full year in business was what I now affectionately refer to as "revenue free"! That's a nice way of saying it took me 12 months to land my first customer. With a family to support, I had to find a way to avoid going further into debt if possible while keeping my entrepreneurial dream alive. That brought me to my next gutsy move: borrowing money to keep the business afloat.

For many entrepreneurs, and this may include you, this might mean borrowing against your credit cards. Using a credit card is a quick way to keep paying your bills, but it is also emotionally difficult for many people.

There were countless Fridays (my bill-paying day) that I had to dig up another credit card and charge what was needed in order to stay afloat for another week. The conversation in my head went something like this: "Okay, Jim, this is the last time we're doing this. We're going to get some new clients this week and start paying off this mountain of credit card debt... or else."

If you are in this situation now, know that I feel your pain and understand completely. Nobody likes credit card debt. Here are a few things that I did that got me over the mental hurdle, and sometimes, anguish, of charging things like my mortgage and food on a credit card while I was working on establishing my business.

1. First, I stopped referring to it as "borrowing on my credit cards or credit card debt." I hated this feeling so much that I had to find a way to make it palatable. So I started to refer to each transaction as either drawing down my "business line of credit," or I referred to the balance on each credit card as "a business loan." You see, it's not uncommon for any business to have business loans, so I had several with various banks that chose to lend me money – essentially believing in my entrepreneurial dream!

2. I also knew two things in my gut: I was going to be very successful, and I was never going to be anyone's employee ever again. Knowing these facts made it easy for me to borrow what I needed as my company started to grow. In a

way, getting my head straight about this cleared my conscience and moved my mindset from one of "Holy crap, I owe a lot on credit card debt" to "I am one step closer this week to turning the corner on this soon-to-be-very-successful business."

Ultimately, it comes down to believing in yourself and your entrepreneurial dream so strongly that you're willing to do whatever it takes to become successful, and THAT is a gutsy move!

The third stage of "gutsy" arrives after your business has achieved some success and you move from a freewheeling, shoot-from-the-hip management style to that of a more seasoned business owner who is overseeing established systems and procedures. In this stage, entrepreneurs typically grow more conservative or perhaps even downright cautious when making business decisions. There are two reasons for this:

1. You now have increased responsibilities through your business to your family, perhaps even a support staff, and your established customers.
2. If you've experienced being broke, that struggle never leaves your mind, so you make more calculated decisions to ensure the ongoing success that you have now achieved.

Although these reasons may be quite valid, they are wrong, and this conservative stage can stifle additional growth and make you unaware of or unwilling to try new things. My advice: To the best of your ability, always be on the lookout for new growth opportunities, new revenue streams, and new ways to harness your creativity to combine your current knowledge and experience with your once youthful exuberance and "damn the torpedoes" entrepreneurial spirit with which you started.

The second part of "guts" is trusting your intuition. Whether you call it your gut, intuition, the universe, providence, the Holy Spirit, or whatever term you want to use, as an entrepreneur you should trust your gut. When I look back on decisions or plans that didn't go well, truth be told, my gut was "buzzing like a disturbed beehive," warning me not to proceed. However, my heart was saying, "Ignore that old conservative gut and plow full steam ahead, you brave entrepreneur!" Of course, I should have listened to my gut.

As a reasonably seasoned business owner, I have learned to trust my gut 99% of the time. Whether it's a major decision or even one as seemingly simple as taking on a new client, pause and check in with yourself about whether it feels right, and you will likely get the right answer.

Of course the hard part for many entrepreneurs is that in our heads and in our hearts we want a new client so badly that we'll often take one that sounds too good to be true... and you know what they say about things that are too good to be true. We get so excited about the new cash flow that this client represents that we overlook the "buzzing" in our guts, only to find out that, yes, they were too good to be true. They only order half of what they promised, and they don't pay you on time, always promising that with the next job you do, they'll get current.

So the bottom line is this: Be gutsy and pursue your dreams, but trust your gut along the way!

Persistence

Nothing is more essential than the willingness to be persistent and keep going, even in your darkest hour. This is true in any endeavor, but it is especially true when launching and running your business.

Despite struggling, you never know how close you might be to real success. The book, *Three Feet from Gold*, by Sharon Lector and Greg Reid, really drives this point home, and it's a book I recommend. I can really relate to this powerful lesson.

Imagine if, after my first 11 months in business and not getting one paying client in that time, I gave up, refusing to tap one more credit card to make it one more week. Those were dark days to be sure, but what I didn't know was that I was very close to getting not just my first client but several more as well. All the seeds I had been planting for 11 months were getting ready to produce the harvest. I hate to think about where I might be if I had quit. Certainly, I would not have the successful businesses I have today, so my strong advice to you is: don't quit!

Being a man of faith, I also believe that God is constantly testing us. During those initial dark days of my business, I kept imagining God saying to me, "I'm not sure you really want this bad enough, Jim. Show me that you have the persistence to keep working, keep making one more phone call, to keep going to one more network event... prove it to me."

"Never, never, never give up."
~ Winston Churchill

If you need more inspiration about being persistent in the face of adversity, I'll recommend *It's Okay To Be Scared But Never Give Up,* the book I co-authored with Martin Howey. In addition to our stories, you can read the stories of nine other highly successful business owners and the challenges they faced and how they overcame them.

Strategy

No matter what your business may be, whether you sell a product or service, it is essential that you have a clear and focused strategy for success.

Step one in creating a strategy is to have a business plan. Now you might be breaking out into a sweat reading those words. Many fear that business plans are complicated and difficult. A business plan doesn't have to be either one of those things – you can find plenty of templates and how-to information with a basic Internet search. The point is you really do need a business plan.

Your business plan will serve as the map or GPS coordinates that you will need to guide you to success. Creating a business plan will help you uncover the needs and desires that you should be filling in order to have a successful enterprise. Think back to all the examples I shared in Chapter 2. You can be certain that those successful entrepreneurs all had a plan. A solid business plan will help you clearly understand and discover your purpose, your values, your mission, and your vision.

By going through the process of creating a business plan, you'll also be able to see where your weaknesses may be and who your competition may be so that you can correct those issues before you even get started. You can also delineate opportunities and threats, taking advantage of the former and avoiding the latter.

Target Audience

Knowing exactly who your target audience is and knowing your market are more important than the product you sell or the service you offer. Please re-read that sentence: *Knowing exactly who your target audience is and knowing your market are more important than the product you sell or the service you offer.*

Don't skimp over this aspect of building your business plan. You want to know with intense hyper clarity and specificity who your perfect target customer is. You should know how old they are, their gender, their occupation, the type of neighborhood they live in. Why? If you don't know this information, you will never reach them with any type of marketing you do.

I'll let you in on a secret: When I'm shooting my weekly videos for my web-based TV show, called Newsletter Guru TV (www.NewsletterGuru.tv), and looking into the camera lens, I'm actually thinking about and picturing a single person, not the thousands of entrepreneurs who watch each week. I keep their image in my head and have a one-on-one conversation with them as I'm shooting the video. I also know some marketers who post a photo of the person who most represents their target audience next to their desks while they're writing copy or devising marketing plans.

All great marketing should be one-to-one communication. We all want to be special and be the center of attention. Your customers, clients, or patients want to be the focus of your message. That won't happen if you handle your marketing (whether you're writing copy, shooting videos, tweeting, or posting on social media) as if you are addressing everyone on your list at the same time, whether your list contains 100 or 100,000 names. Target the message to a single individual – the right individual. And you can only know who the right individual is if you've done your homework and truly know your market. Be certain you nail down that critical information while developing your business plan.

Like I said, your business plan is your map, and if you don't know where you're going, any road will get you there. However, that haphazard approach rarely, if ever, leads to success.

Your business plan will provide you with an overall strategy for your business: who you are, what you do (or what you offer), and what makes you unique. Plus you will understand who your best target audience is and the best way to reach them. As part of your plan, you'll also outline your marketing strategies to attract a steady stream of new clients, customers, or patients.

The most important thing about a business plan is that it's a dynamic document. It's not something that you'll create, refer to in the initial days of your business, and then shove in a drawer or into a computer folder and forget about it. That would be like using a map or GPS at the start of your journey, and then putting the map in the glove compartment or turning off the GPS and expecting to successfully reach your destination.

As your business grows and new opportunities evolve, you should refer to your business plan in your decision-making process and continually tweak and update the document.

So now it's time to turn on your GPS – guts, persistence, and strategy – and start moving toward success. It's time to get started because, remember, it's never going to get easier. The best time to start is right now.

Stop Waiting and Get Going:

❖   Your GPS – guts, persistence, strategy – is the game changer.

❖   You need two kinds of "guts": The guts or courage to start your business and the wisdom to trust your "gut" when making decisions. Your gut instinct is almost always 100% accurate.

❖   Be persistent. The truth is you never know how close you are to real success.

❖   Also, be determined in your persistence. It's a self-fulfilling prophecy. Believe it and it happens.

❖   Strategy is critical, and it comes in the form of a business plan. Take the time to create one and be sure to use it and refer to it.

❖   Make certain you are crystal clear about your target audience and market. Address every marketing communication to one very specific individual who represents your target.

 Success Tips and Gems

"Persistence isn't using the same tactics over and over. Persistence is having the same goal over and over." ~ Seth Godin

71

Develop your brand and USP (unique selling proposition) and be very clear about what sets you apart from your competitors. You want to have your prospects respond with, "Oh yeah, he's the..." or "She's the one who..." and fill in the blank whenever they hear your name. Jim Palmer? Oh yeah, he's the Newsletter Guru.

When you focus on serving others and provide real value and solutions, growth and profits will follow, in any economy. Focus on getting customers and making sales and the opposite will likely occur. The first strategy requires more patience and determination, but in the end you'll have a much stronger business that not only weathers economic downturns, it will be worth more when it's time to cash out.

Never ever give up. Successful entrepreneurs are risk takers; they have the courage to take on new challenges and most importantly, they never give up. You can count on it getting scary, but trust your instincts, keep moving forward, and never give up!

Chapter Eight:
Strategies for Success

As I've stated, it is not my intention to walk you through the nitty-gritty details of launching a business in this book. The things like the type of business to create, whether you should incorporate or operate as a sole proprietorship, and dealing with tax, certification, and licensing issues. There are plenty of books and online information you can refer to for that information.

Instead, I want to share with you some strategies that I have used to become really profitable. After all, profitability defines success. You may offer a product or service about which you are more passionate than anyone else on the planet, but if you can't turn a profit and see bottom-line results, you won't be in business for very long, and you may end up working for someone else again, trading your precious hours for dollars.

Plus, if you find yourself coming out of an unemployment scenario (as I was), it is critical to get up and running *profitably* as quickly as possible!

Risk Reversal

Risk reversal is one of my all-time favorite profit-boosting strategies. When I coach entrepreneurs and small business owners, I always discuss the importance of risk reversal; however, it's critically important when you are starting your business.

When you are starting out, you really don't have a track record about which to boast to your prospects. Chances are also good that you have no testimonials yet. Your prospects have no reason to trust you, and skepticism is high on the list of reasons customers don't say yes to your product or service. Zig Ziglar always emphasized that one of the five main obstacles to a sale is the lack of trust.

Many entrepreneurs and business owners believe that prospects don't buy because of price. High price is *rarely* the reason a prospect doesn't buy even from a long-standing or well-established business. Customers don't buy from businesses that they don't know, like, and trust, and the best way to build trust is to reverse the risk.

You've probably had your own experience with warranties and know that the product will invariably stop working the day, week, or month after the warranty expires. Prospects will hesitate to buy because of that "what if" factor. What if it doesn't work? What if it doesn't deliver as promised? What if I'm not satisfied? It's up to you to eliminate that

Rock-solid gurantee = complete risk reversal, more customers, more profit.

concern. And you can do that by reversing the risk. That is, you, as the business owner, assume all risk associated with the purchase of your product or service.

It's not good enough to offer a 30-, 60-, or 90-day warranty. Your prospect will still be worried about what happens if something goes wrong on the 91st day or even 120th day. If they're wondering about that, they're going to hesitate to buy, especially from someone running a relatively new or just-launched business. Make your guarantee ironclad and super strong, and you will show that you are completely confident in what you are offering.

When you are completely confident in your product or service, you have nothing to lose by offering a rock solid guarantee. Quite the opposite. You have everything to gain: more sales and higher profits.

I know that many business owners worry about being taken by offering a really strong guarantee, and honestly, I can't say that will *never* happen. However, I truly believe that 98 percent of your prospects will be and are honest. You will increase sales and boost your profits by catering to the 98 percent and not worrying about the two percent who might be looking for something for nothing.

Along those same lines, never overlook the lifetime value of your customers, clients, or patients. It is worth far, far more than the refund they may be seeking. Here's a great example of that:

I recently had this very experience with my cell phone carrier. While riding in the car, I couldn't get a signal, so I called the carrier and was told that all three of my lines showed that they were in signal range. Three? I had cancelled the third line almost two years prior, and now only had one for my wife and one for me. I queried the representative further and discovered that this third line had racked up $200 in charges since the time I had cancelled it, and he had the documentation of my cancellation request! When he offered a paltry $20 credit and explained that he wasn't authorized to do more, I asked to be connected with his manager or someone who did have extended authorization. She got on the line and up'd the credit to $100. Before I go any further with this story, let me tell you that I had been a faithful customer to this carrier for more than a dozen years. I asked her to verify my contract expiration which was coming due in two months. With that information, I suggested that unless I was credited the full amount (generated by the vendor's admitted error!), I would terminate my relationship with them. She finally agreed, hopefully because she weighed the value of a $200 credit against the value of my continued revenue.

Never overlook lifetime value!

The bottom line of this strategy: Offer quality and back it up. Leave no doubt in your prospect's mind that all of the risk is on you. And for goodness sake, make sure you clearly understand the lifetime value your customers, clients, or patients bring to your business or practice. Don't nickel and dime them over something trivial.

Positioning

When making a comparison, you know how important it is to compare apples to apples, right? There are plenty of apples out there, so you want to be sure your business looks like a big, juicy orange. In this metaphor, apples represent a commodity, and no matter what business you're in, you don't want to be perceived as a commodity.

Commodities equal low prices. Commodities are the proverbial "dime a dozen," and if your business is perceived as a commodity, the only way to get clients to buy from you is to offer low pricing. Low pricing never translates to high profits. Customers who buy based on price rarely stick around; as soon as another vendor offers a lower price, they switch.

One of the foundations of business success is customer retention. You work hard to gain new customers, clients or patients, and once you have them, you want to keep them. Your repeat customers are your most profitable ones. They spend more with you, and you ultimately spend less on them. (This is such an important concept that I've written a whole book about it: *Stick Like Glue – How to create an everlasting bond with your customers so they spend more, stay longer and refer more!*)

You will never win the customer-retention battle when you have to spend all of your time waging a commodity-based price war. You have to figure out how to eliminate the apples-to-apples comparison by setting yourself apart as a big, juicy orange instead.

Figure out how you can set yourself apart by adding value to your service or product and by offering something that your competitors do not. Make that the focus of your marketing message. When you offer more value, you won't get stuck in the trenches of the price wars.

One way to do this ties right back into what we were just talking about regarding risk reversal. Many times a rock solid, no-questions-asked, money-back guarantee is enough to set yourself apart. As an example, back in my bike shop days, I offered a lifetime guarantee that exceeded the manufacturer's warranty. My competitors thought I was crazy, but this lifetime guarantee set us apart and because of it, we sold a lot of bikes. A lot of 'em.

This approach also went a long way in solidifying customer retention. Customers returned to us time and time again for other products and for bikes for other family members simply because of

Strive to be a big, juicy orange in a world of everyday apples.

the guarantee we offered. We were creating customers for life, and customers for life are worth their weight in gold.

Think hard about your business. There may be something very valuable that's apparent to you but that your customers don't know about. Don't take that for granted. Talk about it so you can set yourself apart and charge what your worth. Never be afraid of the cost of adding value. I guarantee that what you spend on additional value will continue to provide a very profitable return on your investment.

Listen, Learn, and Profit

As a business owner or entrepreneur, you need LLP. And by that I don't mean limited liability partnership. The LLP I'm talking about isn't a legal description, but it's one of the most profitable-building business strategies I know. LLP is Listen, Learn, and Profit.

Chances are good that you will launch or have launched your business with an idea of where you want to go and what you want your business to be. There's nothing wrong with that. In fact, if you didn't have that initial idea, you shouldn't be launching a business in the first place. That said, it's important to really listen to your customers and what they want and need. What they tell you may cause you to change direction, or it may open up other avenues to increase your business.

My own enterprise is a perfect example. I started by writing and designing newsletters for clients who told me their main pain point was that they never knew what to write about or they didn't have the time to do it themselves. By listening to them, I realized I could start another revenue stream, and I launched No Hassle Newsletters (www.thenewsletterguru.com) by creating content that my customers could use in their company newsletters – what I now refer to as my "Famous Customer-Loving™ Content."

From there, customers told me about a new pain: they struggled to create good newsletter design and couldn't afford to hire a graphic artist. From listening to those comments, I added another benefit: my "done for you" No Hassle Newsletter templates. After that, I made sure I listened again when my customers told me about the difficulties they were having printing and mailing their newsletters, so I created and launched The Newsletter Guru's Concierge Print and Mail On-Demand Service (www.newsletterprintingservice.com).

As technology evolved, I heard from customers talking about the difficulty of leveraging and keeping up with social media campaigns. You guessed it: I launched No Hassle Social Media (www.nohasslesocialmedia.com)!

To effectively listen and learn, you have to get out where your customers are and ask! In the previous examples, I heard about my customers' problems and pain points when I interacted with them at both face-to-face meetings and at various networking events. You have to actively seek feedback from your customers, or you are unlikely to get it.

The feedback your customers provide is the gold nugget you need in order to figure out how to sell more to your existing customers. Remember, your existing customers, clients, or patients are your most valuable ones. They already know, like, and trust you; you don't have to spend time and resources marketing to and selling them. Once they've established a relationship with you, your customers want to buy from you, so you have to continually listen and learn in order to keep selling new services to grow your revenue and increase your profits.

Focus on Retention

Retention is truly one of the building blocks of creating a successful business. As I mentioned, it's so important that it is the total focus of one of.my earlier books, *Stick Like Glue – How to create an everlasting bond with your customers so they spend more, stay longer and refer more!* Of course, I think that's worth reading in its entirety, but I want to take a few minutes to touch on it here.

To start, I want to explain the 80/20 rule. It's actually very simple: 80 percent of your profits come from 20 percent of your customers. Yes, you read that correctly. 80 percent of your profits come from 20 percent of your customers. I hope you *immediately* realize with that information how critically important your existing and best customers truly are to you. They are worth every effort!

It takes work, effort, and resources to gain a new customer. As we've already covered, you have to work to overcome the "know, like, and trust" hurdle in order to convert a prospect to a customer. That effort and the resources you dedicate to it make up the cost of acquisition, and the cost of acquisition can be staggering. It actually costs about five times more to acquire a new customer than it does to retain an existing one.

Too many businesses make the mistake of constantly trying to market to new customers rather than applying time and energy to their existing ones. They work and spend like crazy to make the initial sale, and after that single transaction, they go back to focusing on finding another new customer. That's crazy! They've actually gotten someone to open their wallet and spend money with them which is the single biggest hurdle of converting a prospect to a customer. They actually have their foot in the door, but instead of working to open that door wider, they go look for another door that they'll have to pry open from the start.

In addition to the 80/20 rule, I'd like to share another one with you: the 1% = 7% principle. Research shows that for every one percent you increase your customer retention rate, you'll increase your profits by seven percent. Pay special attention, I said profits not revenue. That's huge! An increase of seven percent right to your bottom line, right into your wallet. That principle really underscores the importance of the

Your current customers are a gold mine. Do everything to keep them and watch profits soar!

lifetime value of a customer. Looking back at the experience I had with my cell phone carrier, if I had ultimately canceled my contract because of dissatisfaction, they would have lost a great deal more than the $200 refund.

So now you're nodding your head with an appreciation for the importance of customer retention, but you may be thinking, "That's great Jim, but what do I do to keep my customers?" The answer is very simple: over-the-top customer service. Always under promise and over deliver. It's a surefire way to add a "wow" value that will keep your customers coming back over and over and, even better, refer your business to their friends, family, and colleagues.

Never hesitate to go above and beyond for every one of your customers. Make sure that every touch point you have with them whether it's email, voicemail, or in person is extremely positive. Make sure your website is easy to navigate and that your brick-and-mortar business is clean and neat as a pin. In a nutshell, be easy to do business with.

Customers will stick with you when you meet their expectations. When you can exceed their expectations, they're far more likely to refer you to others. You know that your existing customers are your most valuable ones. Guess which ones are the second most valuable? It's those prospects who are referred to you by existing customers. A referral already has a reason to trust you – they've heard good things from someone else they trust. I won't tell you that there's no "know, like, and trust" hurdle to get over with a referral; however, it's a much, much lower and easier hurdle to clear.

Go out of your way to over deliver to your existing customers, clients, or patients, and they'll stick with you and increase your profits. Plus, they'll be happy to refer you over and over again.

One More Degree

There's another strategy that I would like to share with you here that will have a huge impact on your new business. It ties into the need for persistence that I covered in the section about business GPS. I shudder to think about where I might be today if I had given up after my first 11 months in business. I might be back in the dreaded routine of trading hours for dollars rather than running my own very successful enterprise. I never talk about my success to boast; I only use it as an example, so you can see what's truly possible for yourself.

There is a book I really love, *212 Degrees, the Extra Degree* by S.L. Parker. It's a quick read, but it carries a very powerful message, and its message reiterates what I said about persistence. Very simply, a small change can make a big difference.

First, think about boiling water. When water is at 211 degrees, not much happens. It takes a lot of energy to get water to that temperature, but it doesn't really generate any results. However, with just a little more energy, we can increase the temperature one more degree to boiling. Boiling water creates steam, and steam changed the world during the Industrial Revolution. Steam power proved to be exponentially more valuable than the energy it took to raise the water temperature one more tiny degree.

Water @ 211°= Very hot water.

Water @ 212°= Power to change the world.

A little bit more energy and effort is often the difference between success and failure. There are countless Olympic and athletic competitions in which the difference between first and second place, or winning a medal and being off the podium, is but a fraction of a second. That fraction of a second represents a little more energy and effort.

The thing is that you never know in your business when you might be sitting at 211 degrees. That's exactly where I was after 11 months when I first started my business. Believe in yourself, the persistent, and continue to push one more degree. Success always comes down to that last degree.

A Lesson on Lists

I'm going to take a few minutes here to give you a short primer on lists – how to go about growing a list and then nurturing your list, so your prospects and customers are not only responsive, they're very profitable.

The information age has made creating and maintaining a list of your prospects and customers more important than ever. Right now you may be thinking, "Wait a minute Jim, I haven't even launched my business yet, and you want to talk about something as specific as having a list."

I can understand why you would think that, and the reason I'm including this information now is just to get you thinking. Delivering top-notch customer service often relies on data. My hope is that by explaining the basics to you now, you may be able to avoid some common mistakes about list building, and that a year from now you don't look back and think, "Gee I wish I had collected that information."

There are four phases of list development. Phase one is pretty much for people starting out and might be anywhere from a handful to a few dozen people. You are in the process of building your business, and you also want to be sure that you're creating your list and keeping data on your customers and prospects. At this point you may have a perceived niche or an angle, but you don't have enough people following you or asking you questions that's going to help you further refine your list and define your message.

Phase two is where you grow from several dozen people to several hundred people. It's growing slowly but steadily. Now you will be at the point where you're getting feedback, and people are responding to your emails and electronic newsletters and other communications that you send. You are starting to learn more about their specific needs, wants, and desires.

Phase three is when your list grows from about 500 people to 1000 people or more. Now you're on target and you know what your message is. You deliver it with consistency and regularity, and now it's going to be time to kick it up a notch. At this point, you have probably started getting new clients from your list who had only been prospects before.

The final phase of list building is when your list grows to thousands and thousands or even tens of or hundreds of thousands. There's no doubt that you can have $1 million business on a list of 10,000 people. But that doesn't necessarily mean that a list of 50,000 or 100,000 is going to automatically bring you multiples of millions of dollars in revenue. It's important to always be cognizant of who is on your list and why they are following you.

As your business (and hence your list) is growing, you want to be very aware of tracking your customers' interests. This is especially important if you are offering various products or services. Having this data lets you intelligently cross sell and refine your marketing message so that it speaks directly and relevantly to your audience. Remember the importance of knowing and understanding your target audience as we covered in the last chapter.

Business intelligence is born of data. Your customers, clients, or patients are the ones who dictate what they will buy from you. You could start your business with the vision of selling Widget A, and you might have the best darn Widget A on the planet and be the best darn Widget A salesperson ever. However, if the folks on your list are more interested in Widget B, you're never going to have a growing, profitable business.

In order to provide what your customers want, you have to collect and pay attention to data.

More Strategies

Now is really a great time to start your business. Every day that you procrastinate puts you another day further from your dream business, but as I said, your dream business must be profitable in order to sustain you and create your own economic boom.

The handful of strategies I've shared with you in this chapter are ones that I believe you need to learn and embrace in order to make your new business as profitable as possible as quickly as possible. However, these are simply the tip of the iceberg.

There are many more strategies that I use in my business to keep it highly profitable and constantly growing. You can read more about these in my book, *The Fastest Way to Higher Profits! 19 Immediate Profit Enhancing Strategies You Can Use Today.*

Plus, I offer a lot of nuts and bolts, profit-building building information in my Summer Business School sessions, (www.JimsBusinessSchool.com), through one-on-one coaching, (check out my mastermind and coaching opportunities at www.TheNewsletterGuru.com) or by listening to my my Stick Like Glue Radio podcast. You can subscribe to it at iTunes and www.GetJimPalmer.com.

Stop Waiting and Get Going:

❖ Eliminate your prospects' worries about your product or service. Put all the risk on yourself, provide a quality product or service, and offer a rock solid guarantee.

❖ Don't be a commodity. Set your business apart as a big, juicy orange in a sea of apples, and you will not have to battle in the trenches of low-price warfare. You can charge and receive what you're worth.

❖ Ask for feedback from your customers and then listen to it and learn from it. They will provide you with the exact information you need in order to grow your business, create new products or services, and expand your revenue streams.

❖ Above all else, customer retention is the key to higher profits. Spend plenty of time, energy, and resources on your existing customers, clients, or patients.

❖ Be persistent and keep pushing. A little more effort and energy may be all that's needed to change your business and the world.

❖ Be mindful of the importance of collecting data about your customers, clients, or patients from the day you launch your business or practice. Pay attention to what that data tells you.

Success Tips and Gems

Treat customers like family – or better! I think Sam Walton said it best: "There is only one boss - the customer. And he can fire everybody in the company from the chairman on down, simply by spending his money somewhere else."

When is the last time you said or showed your customers, clients, or patients how much you appreciate them? Work every day to increase loyalty and retention. It's the fastest way to higher profits.

Every business is like a leaky bucket, and it's paramount to your survival that you continuously fill your bucket with more water (customers). After all, no water, no business! A better strategy is to plug the holes in your bucket and keep the customers you have!

Customers don't hesitate to buy because of price; they hesitate to buy because of worry. They worry about all the "what ifs." Remove the risk with a rock-solid guarantee and you'll close more sales.

Referrals reduce your sales expense, sales cycle, are more profitable, and they allow you to focus more time and effort on your current customers. Do you have a referral program?

Often, you might be on the verge of an incredible breakthrough or higher profits but unaware of it. So dig deep and keep pushing it one more degree. Success often comes down to just one more degree!

Two reasons why my first newsletter worked so well: I wrote it in a conversational tone, just the way I would talk to a customer in the store, and I mailed it to every name we had on the store's customer list! Lists matter.

Figure out your value and what value you can add to your product or service: that value eliminates any perception that you're a commodity. If customers perceive you as such, they'll always want to buy on price alone.

Chapter Nine:
Types of Revenue

In the last chapter, I shared with you some key strategies I have employed to make my enterprise profitable and successful. Profits are critical, but you can't have profits until you have revenue. So I'd like to take some time to review the different sources of revenue you might have in your business.

This is pretty foundational stuff, but now that I hopefully have you excited and ready to launch your new business, it's important to build your business on a solid foundation. I want to get you thinking big from the beginning, and I want to give you new ways to think about business. As you are reading this chapter, I want you to keep an open mind and really think about how you can apply this information as you think about launching your business, or if you have already started the business, how you can begin applying this now.

Transactional

There are a lot of business owners who view business success in terms of transactions. They sell one thing to one customer, and then they look to repeat that sale to a new customer or they wait for the original customer to come back and buy again. That's the first type of revenue: transactional income. The vast majority of businesses have transactional income.

Whether you are planning to launch or have launched your business as a brick-and-mortar store, an online store, a print and mail catalog, or anything in between, you'll probably have transactional revenue. A purchase is made or a service is bid on. You deliver the product or you provide the service, and you get paid. That's the transaction, and that's the very nature of transactional business.

This is the most common type of revenue, and it is probably the least valuable. The problem, of course, is that you are constantly searching for new customers with whom to conduct more transactions because unless and until another transaction is made, you have no more revenue coming in. There are many businesses in which 100 percent of the revenue is transactional income. In fact, some of these businesses do a million dollars or more. That's good. But unless they prove that, day in and day out, the transactional income is going to continue, there is no real comfort level or guarantee of success.

Secondly, recurring revenue is a main factor when it's time to sell a business. Now you're probably thinking, "Whoa Jim, I haven't even launched my business yet and now you're talking about selling it." Like I said, I want to get you thinking about the big picture and every aspect of running your business. If you rely solely on transactional income as your only source of revenue, you will work harder and have more stress running your business, and when it does come time to sell years down the road, you will find that a business that operates completely on transactional income will not be worth as much as a business that enjoys other types of revenue. So let's talk about those.

Repeat

The second type of revenue is repeat income, and this is where transactions are, by their very nature, repeatable. The simplest type of repeatable income is gained by providing a quality product or service that your customers, clients, or patients require over and over. For example, if you operate a carpet cleaning service and do an outstanding job, your customers will probably have you come back every year or even a few times per year. That's repeatable income.

Let me segue for a moment and touch on building good relationships with your customers. You can provide the greatest service in world, but unless you develop a relationship with your customers, there's no guarantee that they are going to remember you. Imagine this: ABC Carpet Cleaning does a fantastic job at the Palmer household and gets out every single stain. The carpets look like new. A year later, when the Palmers need carpet cleaning again, they may or may not remember that it was ABC Carpet Cleaning that did such a stellar job... unless ABC develops a relationship with the Palmers.

On the other hand, if ABC stays in touch with them by making a follow-up phone call in six months, or better stays in

Focus on the 3 R's of revenue:

- *Repeatable*
- *Renewable*
- *Recurring*

more regular and frequent contact, the Palmers will not forget who did such a great job cleaning the carpets and will be quick to contact them when their services are needed again. Of course I firmly believe that newsletters are one of the best ways to stay in regular and frequent contact with your customers, clients, or patients. It's a great way to create a relationship, and a good relationship coupled with a great product or service leads to repeatable income. That's good. No, that's great.

For the many businesses that rely on transactional income, smart business owners are striving to make those transactions repeatable. Another good example of this is home heating oil. I've been with the same home heating company for 20 years. Every year, I get a contract that states, "If your burner breaks down we're going to come out within one day for repairs and offer X number of dollars (or a percentage) off of replacement parts." That's a way of locking me in and knowing that they can rely on repeat revenue from me. Of course, they have to offer great service as a starting point.

Renewable

The third type of revenue is renewable income. This is essentially repeat income that is guaranteed by pre-arrangement or pre-agreement. Insurance is a good example of renewable revenue. If you sell someone an insurance policy, it typically renews year after year automatically. You don't have to go out and re-sell the policy every single year.

While I am only scratching the surface of this, I hope it's enough to get you thinking, "How can I use this in my business? What can I do to set it up so that I move from transactional income to repeat income? And then how can I convert repeat income to renewable income?"

Recurring

The final type of revenue that I want to cover with you is the most important one especially for small business owners. It's continuity income or recurring income. In a continuity program, your customer will have agreed when they engaged your service or made a purchase that there will be automatic renewals or redeliveries at specified time intervals. Almost 99 percent of these are credit-card based, so automated payment is ensured.

Some of the products that you may see on infomercials, like the acne medicine Proactive, are sold as continuity programs. Some of these are forced continuity programs in which you must establish ongoing deliveries when you make the initial purchase. Some subscription services may also be forced continuity in so much that the customer has to take steps to suspend it, or it automatically renews for another year. While you always have the opportunity to opt out, you must establish a renewal schedule from the start.

Some of my programs, including No Hassle Newsletters and No Hassle Social Media, are continuity programs. My customers make a decision to continue at the time of the initial sale. It's not forced continuity; however, they know they're signing up for a monthly program. They know they're going to get great newsletter or social media content month after month.

Customers in both of these cases, whether it's continuity or forced continuity, must proactively take the initiative to cancel the program. The beauty of continuity income is that every month you know to some degree what your income will be. And the even greater benefit is that many businesses in many industries lend themselves to continuity programs! Over the years, I've talked to many entrepreneurs and have coached business owners who have almost always been able to develop some sort of continuity program, even in businesses in which you might not think it was possible.

I know someone is in the pizza business, running Diana's Gourmet Pizza. She developed a continuity program for her pizza club and offers three different levels. It's really pretty simple: there's a $35-, a $50-, and a $75-a-month program. For each level, she gives out more in pizza bucks to spend in the store than the value of the chosen program. For example, if you're in the $35-a-month program, you get $50 in pizza bucks. Every month, she knows how many people are in which program and what she can count on as reliable, continuous revenue.

But here's something more to think about: You have Joe's Pizza on one corner and Diana's Gourmet Pizza on the other corner. Joe is pounding out coupons every month through Value Pack and similar distribution channels. At the beginning of every month, Joe is trying to figure out how much revenue he might get from his coupons, what the return on his investment will be, and how he can bring in more business. At the same time on the other corner, Diana is simply hitting 100 credit cards for $35. That's

$3500 a month plus the revenue she generates from her higher valued programs.

If you knew that you had already purchased either $50, $75, or $100 of Diana's pizza bucks, are you going to shop someplace else for pizza? I doubt it. Of course it's a given that Diana makes great pizza – the kind people want to return for again and again. This type of program is similar to those used by smart restaurant owners who promote birthdays and offer you a free meal on your birthday. Nobody goes out to dinner on their birthday by themselves; they always take someone along. In this promotion your meal is free, but guess what? All the rest of the food and beverages are not covered, so by offering one free meal, the restaurant owner increases revenue. Diana has shared with me that her customers always spend more than the number of pizza bucks she awards. If someone gets $50 a month, they typically spend much more than that, and it's an absolute moneymaker.

Unless you happen to know Diana, I doubt that you would have figured that a pizza business could create a continuity program. And that's really the point – no matter what business you are thinking about creating or have already created, I want you to look at it differently and try to determine how you can create a continuity program. First and foremost, that is one of the most important things you can do. It not only improves your comfort level by having a good sense of the monthly revenue you can expect, it will also make a huge difference when you decide it's time to retire and you want to sell your business. A business that has regular recurring revenue is exponentially more valuable when it's time to sell.

Revenue Streams

Another important factor to consider when creating and launching your business is to look for multiple revenue streams. When I started my business over 10 years ago, I was working one-on-one with individual corporations, associations, nonprofits, and chambers of commerce writing, designing and printing their newsletters. I was always happy to get paid, of course, but I knew I then had to go and find my next client. It really wreaked havoc on my schedule, and after about five years, my wife asked if we were ever going to go on vacation again. My first thought was that she was right, but my second thought was, "How can I leave the business? I'm the chief cook and bottle washer."

Multiple revenue streams let you turn your business into a more profitable enterprise!

I knew that if I wasn't there nothing moved, nothing got done, nobody met with the client, and nobody did the billing. That's when I started to transition my business to create multiple revenue streams. So now I have my membership programs, both of which are continuity based, so there's a certain amount of revenue that comes in every single day whether I'm here or not.

Let me share something important with you about that: I don't do monthly billing; everything doesn't happen on the first day of the month. Whenever someone signs up for a program, no matter what day of the month it happens to be, that's when their 30-day cycle begins. If they happen to sign up on the eighth of the month, their payment will always be due on the eighth of every month. That billing model lets me have continuous income and helps reduce cash flow problems.

As I have shared with you in this and my other books, I have expanded my operation from where I started. In addition to newsletters and the No Hassle Newsletter program, I have my publishing business, my printing business, my social media program, my coaching business, and informational marketing products such as Double My Retention, the MARS training program (Magnetic Attraction and Retention System), Jim Palmer's Summer Business School, and Coaching Program. You can find more information on all of these at my virtual storefront, www.JimsProfitCenter.com. On any given day if, for whatever reason, I lose clients or revenue from one part of my enterprise, there are plenty of other revenue streams I can count on.

I want you to begin thinking about how you can create multiple revenue streams in your business and how you can have different types of income rolling in. It's okay to start with transactional revenue as most businesses do, but be certain that you are also looking for repeat and renewable income, but most of all, you really want to be working toward the granddaddy of them all – continuity income.

Stop Waiting and Get Going:

❖ Transactional income may be the starting point for your business, but always look for ways to convert transactional income into repeat income.

❖ Repeat and renewable incomes are impossible unless you provide a fantastic product or service and back that up with over-the-top customer service.

❖ The number one, best type of income to have in your business is continuity revenue – automatically renewed income. It makes running the business easier and increases your comfort level since you'll have some degree of knowledge about your income every month.

❖ It might seem crazy to think about selling your business when you are starting out, but that day will come, and businesses with continuity revenue are exponentially more valuable.

❖ Increase the number of revenue streams you have: It helps eliminate cash flow problems and reliance on a single product line for your income. If there's a downturn in one, you have others to support you.

 Success Tips and Gems

Don't celebrate transactions. Celebrate healthy, dependable, reliable, predictable, profitable client relationships!

Do at least one thing every day to generate current revenue and plant seeds for future revenue. Both are critically important.

When you lose a customer, you don't just lose a line in your mailing list! You lose all future sales and referrals (and those future sales and referrals) ... and on and on it goes!

Successful entrepreneurs usually don't focus on sales. They generally focus on how to provide greater value to their customers, knowing the profits will follow.

Profit Tip: If you're not getting pricing resistance from 20 to 30 percent of your prospects, your prices are likely too low!

Most businesses focus too much energy on transactional income. What's more important (and valuable) is repeat income, renewable income, and continuity income.

Gross is for vanity, net is for sanity.

If you're not earning enough, ask yourself this question: When was the last time you increased the value and level of service that you're providing? Whether you're an employee or entrepreneur, the answer is the same. The best chance to increase your 'earnings' (key word) is to serve others and find ways to provide more value.

Make sure all your marketing doesn't scream "transactions wanted!"

About Price Elasticity, How Much Is Too Much? If you're not getting some occasional complaints that your prices are too high, you probably aren't charging enough. If you're winning every job without so much as a question about your pricing, I guarantee your prices are too low and you are not charging what you're worth.

Like you, your customers are not looking for a one-time transaction. Changing vendors, companies, or brands is usually a hassle, just like looking for more new customers! Make sure that your marketing and ways of doing business project that you will be there to support them long term. Bonus Tip: If you do this, you'll instantly stand above 90% of your competition.

Even though you built your business from the ground up as chief cook and bottle washer, if you really want to achieve substantial (and faster) growth, you must 'let go' of all non high-revenue producing tasks.

Chapter Ten:
Consider Coaching

I bet there have been various points in your life when you used a coach. Maybe it goes as far back as a stint in high school athletics, music, or drama. Maybe even further back than that, like Little League or youth soccer. Or perhaps it's more recent, like golf, tennis, or any other type of lesson you might have taken more recently. Plus you probably had a mentor early in your career, someone who showed you the ropes in your company or in your industry.

Having a coach as you launch your business is very worthwhile. It is an investment you make in yourself and in your future growth and profitability. In most cases, you will find that hiring a coach pays a handsome return on your investment. The coach's job is not just to teach and direct but also to inspire, encourage, and occasionally, as I like to say, offer some 'tough love.' If you peruse many inspirational quotations (and you may even have some posted by your desk), I'm willing to bet that the majority of them were uttered by famous *coaches*.

"A man can be as great as he wants to be. If you believe in yourself and have the courage, the determination, dedication, the competitive drive and if you are willing to sacrifice the little things in life and pay the price for the things that are worthwhile, it can be done."

That statement really sums up one of the main points and one of the main reasons I have chosen to write this book. I'd like to take credit for such an eloquent statement, but I have to give credit where credit is due. Those are Vince Lombardi's words. Like I said, a coach's job is to inspire as well as to teach, but their real impact goes beyond the inspirational speeches they may deliver at game time. A good coach will challenge you, and in the end, I truly believe that while the investment may require some guts, it will prove to be a very wise and profitable decision.

It's All About Mindset

A good business coach can certainly share with you plenty of information about successful strategies to run your business. He or she will have answers to your questions and may even provide answers to questions that you haven't thought to ask. One of the most important things a good coach will do is change your mindset.

I'm a firm believer that, in most cases, our mindset is what holds us back. Everyone at one time or another can be a victim of their own limiting beliefs. It's a self-fulfilling prophecy. I know that was one of the problems I faced when I first started my business.

I was very fortunate to meet a guy, a very successful entrepreneur, who took me under his wing and served as my mentor when I was starting my business. We used to go out to breakfast or lunch frequently, and very early on he asked, "Hey Palmer, what's your dream? What are you going to do with this thing you called Dynamic Communication? What's your vision for Dynamic?"

My answer: "Well John, it's very simple. I'm creating a business that's going to generate $50,000 in revenue, and man, I'm just going to be so happy." I answered with pride because I was only three or four months into my efforts and was thrilled at the prospect of running my own business. I now had a job after over a year of unemployment, and I knew that if I could earn $50,000 in revenue, that would be pretty cool.

You can imagine my surprise when John took me to task and, pardon the expression, bitch-slapped me across the table. His retort: "Jim, what the hell? $50,000? That's ridiculous. What's wrong with $150,000? What's wrong with a half million dollars? Jim, that's ridiculous. That is SO small time."

I could feel my ears turning red, and I was really quite embarrassed. He bluntly pointed out that I had a problem with my mindset. I needed to think bigger, and he challenged me to grow my business bigger. Although my reference to $50,000 was net income not total revenue, it was still mouse droppings, and John helped me see that I needed to broaden my mindset and increase my expectations.

Good coaches teach, inspire, allow you to see bigger and greater possibilities, and kick your butt.

John was the first person to inspire me to 'think bigger,' and it was at this time that I first read Napoleon Hill's classic, *Think and Grow Rich* and also *Psycho-Cybernetics, A New Way to Get More Living Out of Life,* by Maxwell Maltz. It was in these books that I learned about mind movies. I learned to sit in a quiet room with absolutely no distractions, close my eyes, and pretend that I was in a movie theater all by myself, sitting in the back row top center. I was to imagine that the screen was my life and let my mind play out what my life would look after I had half a million dollars. I soon began to see everything I was dreaming of, playing out on the big screen in front of me. When the mind movie was over, I would then write it all down and get working on implementing it.

I'll be the first to admit that it felt a little weird, but I was very surprised when I started doing it at how utterly clear, valuable, and crisp the ideas were. I basically asked the question, "What do I need to do to have a half million dollar business?" And I started getting plenty of ideas. I realized that when I created a newsletter, I didn't just want to get paid a client and then hope and pray that they'd re-order at some point; I wanted to create newsletters that I could have ten, twenty, or even hundreds of people pay me for every month. I loved that idea. I was excited about that idea. I didn't quite know how to do it, but that's okay. I had the idea and I would figure it out!

Over our many months of meetings, John kept pushing me. When I had 35 or 40 clients and I told him my goal was to get to 100, he wanted to know why my goal wasn't 1000. It forced me to expand my mindset again, and my subconscious mind started feeding me the answers I needed. Without having John playing the role of my coach, pushing and inspiring me, I would not be as successful as I am today.

Who's Slapping You Around?

John certainly slapped me around, but it was for my own good. Getting slapped around is no fun, and it's human nature to try to avoid it or retreat as far away from it as you can when it happens. We all want to hang out in our safe zones. It's a rare person who will willingly slap himself or herself around. That's why having a coach is so beneficial.

You definitely want a coach who will challenge you and one who will tell you like it is. We're all very good at letting ourselves off the hook. You want a coach who will force you to be accountable for the actions you take to launch and grow your business. A good coach will never let you off the hook.

As difficult as it might be to hear, you want someone to point out your mistakes and your weaknesses. You want someone to point out the opportunities that you're overlooking. In the words of Peanuts' Lucy from her psychiatrist booth, *"Charlie Brown, it's true. I recognize your frailties and your weaknesses. You need me to point out your faults, Charlie Brown. It's for your own good."*

A good coach will also push you toward goals that you did not think you could achieve. There's a great scene in the movie *Facing the Giants* (2006) in which a high school football coach is challenging one of his linemen to go as far as he can while carrying another player on his back. The player thinks he might be able to make it to the 30-yard line; the coach challenges him to go as far as the 50. In a stroke of genius, the coach then blindfolds him.

Blindfolded and with another player on his back, the lineman struggles down the field with his coach both screaming at and encouraging him. The player continually asks how far he's gone, and his coach continues to disregard his question and urges him to dig deeper and go farther. The player has no idea where he is in relation to his goal. When he finally collapses and removes the blindfold, he sees that he has gone farther than the 30 and farther than the 50; he has, in fact, reached the far end zone.

The player couldn't see his own potential, but his coach could. Even more important, because he couldn't see where he was and thought he had not yet reached his goal, the player continued to dig down and continued to try. Would that have happened or would he have ultimately gone twice as far as he thought even possible without a coach pushing him and encouraging him? Not a chance.

We are all limited by our own perspective of what we may think is possible. Why go it alone? Why try to do it without the encouragement (even when that encouragement may feel like being slapped around) that a good coach can provide. You and your dreams for your business deserve it.

Being a Coach

I hope that you don't make the mistake I almost made in the beginning by thinking too small. I hope that you are like many of my coaching clients in that they are looking for big results. When my coaching clients tell me they are looking for big results, I ask them if they are prepared for their businesses to look completely different than they do today. Let me give you an example, so I can explain what I mean by that.

Let's say your business is jewelry. You're a jeweler; you sell jewelry, and obviously you want to sell as much jewelry as possible. If all you want is to continue selling more and more jewelry, and jewelry sales are your measure of success, that's fine. So with this in mind, you develop some really smart marketing and business-building strategies and drive more people into your store or to your website. Your jewelry sales skyrocket. All's good.

Suddenly other jewelers begin to take notice of you. Maybe you're featured in a trade magazine. Maybe you start to attend conferences and jewelry trade shows. Maybe you win awards for extraordinary sales with a particular watch company. Let's say your revenue is $1.5 million a year while most other jewelers are doing

Establish yourself as the expert and the world just may beat a path to your door.

less than half of that. People are going to notice you, and people are going to begin asking: What are you doing and how are you doing it?

When that happens, whether you realize it or not, you have opened up the opportunity for a new and different revenue stream – coaching. You could begin to offer group coaching calls to share your strategies, and you could offer done-for-you templates of your marketing and advertising pieces. Now in addition to your jewelry sales revenue, you might start adding $40,000 to $50,000 through coaching or a done-for-you marketing program.

You will have set yourself apart as the go-to expert in your industry. The next thing you might want to consider is writing a book about how you achieved your success. It's not unthinkable to have readers seek you out and ask for personal advice. Suddenly you've become a consultant! At this point, like I said, your business looks completely different than when you started. You have various revenue streams, and you are an entrepreneur rather than a small business owner.

You are now on your way to creating recurring revenue, and recurring revenue is an equity driver in your business. Greater equity in your business directly translates to greater wealth. When you get to this point with guts, persistence, and strategy, you will never regret taking the step to launch your business and forever forego trading your precious hours for dollars.

I'm at that point in my enterprise now, and I don't tell you that to brag. I have no doubt that I was a lot like you are right now when I was in the same position. I use myself as an example, so you can clearly see that what I'm suggesting is entirely possible and completely realistic.

Keep in mind that at the core, all businesses are the same. Success is always cut from the same cloth. I strongly encourage you to avoid thinking that coaching won't work for you or your business. Honestly, that's hogwash and narrow-minded thinking. No matter what business you're in, no matter what product you sell or service you offer, I know that having a coach will pay huge dividends on your investment. You will grow exponentially. Never, ever hesitate to invest in yourself, and that's exactly what you're doing when you use a coach!

I spearhead mastermind groups throughout the year and also offer one-on-one coaching. To learn more, I encourage you to visit www.TheNewsletterGuru.com and click on Mastermind and Coaching.

Stop Waiting and Get Going:

❖ You have probably used a coach at other times in your life and career. Finding and hiring a good coach as you launch your business will provide an excellent return on your investment.

❖ A coach will help you change your mindset and achieve more than you ever thought was possible.

❖ We're all very good at letting ourselves off the hook; however, your coach will hold you accountable and make you do the things you say you're going to do.

❖ You will get a better perspective on your shortcomings and ideas on how to overcome them by working with a coach.

❖ Once you are the go-to expert in your field or industry, becoming a coach yourself is an ideal way to generate new revenue streams and expand your enterprise.

 ## Success Tips and Gems

Begin taking action now and don't stop! Positive thinking, goal setting, and even visualization are worthless without one more key ingredient. Action.

"We cannot direct the wind but we can adjust the sails." ~ Dolly Parton (Great quote about controlling your outlook and attitude!)

I appreciate knowledge, skill, resources, etc., but sometimes good old-fashioned 'nose to the grindstone'... 'keep your head down' work also gets the job done!

You will earn higher profits with a business coach. A good coach is not only a source of inspiration and ideas, but also a source of challenge—someone who will push you faster toward profitability.

Two sure fire ways to accelerate your success? 1. Get a business coach. 2. Spend time with smart entrepreneurs who are excelling. Bonus tip 3. Be open-minded to what others are doing. Instead of saying that won't work in my business, ask, "How can I make that work in my business?"

I can't imagine running a business today without a coach or mastermind group. Just when you think you have it figured out, some smarter folks 'reveal' some brilliant ideas that will super charge your growth.

Good Reason to Have a Coach: Entrepreneurs are idea creators, but sometimes it's tough to determine the difference between a great idea and a shiny object. Before you can run down the road full-steam ahead with an idea, bounce it off your coach!

Want to be known as THE 'Go-to Authority' in your field, yet you're still resisting writing a book? Consider that the word 'author' comes from the word 'authority!' Now start writing!

Chapter Eleven: The Power of Thinking Big

As I shared with you in the last chapter, I had a problem with a narrow mindset when I first started my business. I'm forever indebted to John and appreciate how he pushed me to think really big even though it felt an awful lot like getting slapped around at the time. I want to take a little more time delving into the idea of thinking big because I know it will have a huge impact on your business.

Maybe you've heard about the concept of setting SMART goals – goals that are specific, measurable, attainable, realistic, and tangible. I have had any number of coaching clients who, when I pushed them to think bigger than they might have thought possible, question the idea of setting a huge goal that in their minds is neither attainable nor realistic. While I can never speak for what any of them might actually be able to achieve or attain, I am very familiar with the limitations that our brains can place on us when we let them.

Here's a great example of that: Roger Bannister. If that name doesn't ring a bell, let me tell you who he was. Roger Bannister was the first athlete to run a mile in less than four minutes. In 1952 Olympics in Helsinki, Bannister set a British record in the 1500 meters (known as the metric mile); however, he did not win the medal he expected. In fact, he was not even on the podium after the race. With that disappointment, he resolved to become the first person to break the four-minute mile. That was a seemingly insurmountable barrier at the time. No runner had even come close. Bannister wasn't just thinking big, he was thinking *huge*.

Two years later on May 6th, Bannister's big thinking made history when he ran the mile in 3:59.4. You're probably thinking, "Okay, big deal… someone broke a record." But that's not the end of the story. Bannister's amazing record *only stood* for 46 days. Australia's John Landy took nearly two full seconds off his time, running 3:58.0 on June 21st. You see, Bannister did more than run the fastest mile ever at the time; he showed others that the four-minute barrier was

"The man who can drive himself further once the effort gets painful is the man who will win."

~ *Roger Bannister*

really only a matter of a narrow mindset. Once he broke the barrier, the floodgates opened and many other runners were able to complete "sub-four" miles. They saw that it was possible.

I respect those who set SMART goals, but I don't necessarily agree with the attainable and realistic part… thanks to Roger Bannister. He did it first and proved that anything was possible while the rest of the world didn't believe that a sub four-minute mile was attainable or realistic.

Leapfrog

From the time we're born, we're conditioned to believe in taking things one step at a time. We go to first grade, then second grade, then third grade and so on. Every set of instructions comes with step one, step two, step three, etc.

I want to tell you that it doesn't have to be that way. You don't have to climb the ladder one rung at a time. You can achieve more and reach greater success by leapfrogging. Don't be afraid to jump over different steps. Granted, this may not work if you're assembling Ikea furniture, but you're not. You're working on creating a successful business and your own economic boom, and I'm here to tell you that you should leapfrog over different things.

Get ready, get psyched then go from step one and leap over spots two, three, and four, and land on five. It's like the old kids' board game of Chutes and Ladders. Maybe you remember playing it. It was really very simple. The ladders went up and the chutes went down. When you landed at the base of a ladder, up you went. Maybe it was only a single level, but many times it was multiple levels and put you closer to the finish line. Of course, on the other hand, when you landed at the top of a chute, you went down, and there were a few places on the board where you went *all the way down*.

Think about your business like a game of Chutes and Ladders. You want to try to leapfrog levels to become as profitable as possible as soon as possible. Sure, you are going to land on some metaphorical chutes. When that happens, maybe you scream. But pick yourself up, brush yourself off, and start climbing again. Of course, unlike in the game, you can use what you learned to avoid the chutes in the future.

I guarantee that by leapfrogging, and taking your chances with the occasional chute, you are going to reach the top faster than if you plod along with step one, step two, step three... step 157, 158, 159.... you get the point.

Let Your Brain Do the Work

The human brain is an amazing thing, and it can do amazing things when you let it. You simply have to get out of its way by eliminating small thinking and a narrow mindset. John kept pushing me to create a bigger business than I thought possible. I certainly didn't have all the answers or even a clue when he first challenged me, but I gave my brain free rein to brew on the problem of growing my business and coming up with some ideas.

Let's say you're in the business of making and selling quilts. Between the designing, cutting, and stitching, you can turn out and sell one quilt a week. Now I'm going to challenge you and tell you that you have to sell 10 quilts every week. First of all, I don't want you to resist and tell me it's impossible for you to make and sell 10 quilts every week. That's small thinking. Instead, I want you to let

Your brain is an amazing machine. Let it do the hard work and get out of its way!

your subconscious mind start mulling over the problem of how to make 10 quilts a week and start feeding you the answers. It may not come instantly, and in fact, it probably won't. The ideas that hold the answer may come while you're sleeping, while you're driving, or while you're exercising.

Suddenly you realize that you don't have to be the chief sewer of quilts. You could hire other people to make the quilts according to your designs and your specifications. The reality is that you are not going to have a $1 million business or even a $100,000 business if you are the chief sewer of quilts selling one per week… unless of course you are selling them for $20,000 each. You might start out in your business as the chief quilt sewer, but I would love to see you transition yourself into becoming the chief marketer of your incredibly successful quilt-making business.

Don't let your preconceived notions and narrow mindset derail your opportunities for success. Dream big and think big, then let your brain do the work to figure out how to make your dream come true.

Leverage a Mastermind Group

You know that one plus one equals two, right? Now what if I held up two one-dollar bills and told you that one plus one equals

$5, $10, or even $20? I bet you'd pay attention, and the best part is that it's true. That's the power of a mastermind group.

It's a form of synergy that combines forces to create a result that is greater than the sum of its parts. Or more simply, two heads are better than one. To be really successful, you need to hang out with smart people. A well-run mastermind group is your opportunity to do that.

Mastermind groups aren't new. One of the greatest mastermind groups in history was the group of men who had the vision and combined intelligence to launch a revolution and create the new democracy that became the United States. The term "mastermind" is attributed to Napoleon Hill, who coined the phrase in his book *Think and Grow Rich*, first published in 1937.

One of the primary benefits of using a mastermind group is having access to the brain trust that will be at your disposal. As I've said many times in this book, your business is not unique, no matter how much you may think it is. The same thing is true of business challenges and problems – we all have the same ones. Successful entrepreneurs are the ones who find solutions; really successful entrepreneurs are the ones who find the solutions fastest by employing the help of their peers.

Mastermind groups provide you the opportunity to borrow winning practices that you can adapt to using in your own business. The wheel was a great discovery, but there's no point reinventing it over and over again. You want to be spending your precious time growing your business rather than solving problems that have already been solved.

Information, in and of itself, is pretty useless. There's no shortage of information, and it grows exponentially every single day. You have to make sense of the information and put it to use. That's knowledge, and knowledge is power. You'll gain access to knowledge and proven ideas rather than simply collecting information when you participate in a mastermind group.

A mastermind goes well beyond a blended brain trust of knowledge and experience. Every member must bring something to the table. The whole thing would be pretty useless if everyone were there simply to drain knowledge without also making a contribution. The desire to share experiences, proven results, and knowledge is the fuel that propels members of the mastermind forward... and usually at astonishing rates.

Brainstorming sessions create upward spirals of information. If you've ever been in a great brainstorming session, you've experienced this phenomenon. A seemingly ridiculous idea can be molded into a worthwhile and profitable one. One idea builds on another, and the process continues to grow. There's almost always a synergistic result: the outcome is worth more than the total of all the ideas.

One of the other great benefits of the mastermind group is accountability. Like a coach, your mastermind peers will not let you off the hook. No one wants to show up to the group without having done the homework and without some success to brag about. A mastermind group will hold you more accountable than you could ever hold yourself. It's like tough love, and while it may be tough, there's no better place to get the support you need and celebrate success.

I spearhead a number of mastermind groups throughout the course of the year. I love doing it because I get so much out of it and can certainly attest to all of the benefits. To learn more about joining one of my mastermind groups, you can visit www.TheNewsletterGuru.com and click on Mastermind and Coaching.

Stop Waiting and Get Going:

❖ Roger Bannister did more than run the first sub four-minute mile. He proved to the world that it could be done, and once proven, many other athletes completed the same feat shortly thereafter.

❖ Don't obsess about the attainability of your goals. Think big and go for it.

❖ You don't have to proceed toward your goals or success by taking steps one at a time. Try to leapfrog whenever you can to become more profitable faster.

❖ Your brain is an incredible machine. Get out of its way and let your subconscious mind do the work. Then get ready to capture the ideas whenever they come to you – it might be while you're sleeping, driving, or exercising.

❖ Like using a coach, a mastermind group will help you leverage knowledge and make you more successful than going it alone.

❖ Mastermind groups capture the power of synergy. Two heads are better than one. A group of really smart entrepreneurs is best of all.

 Success Tips and Gems

Two huge benefits of being in a mastermind group: tons of fresh ideas and also the opportunity to be around positive 'make it happen' people! Very refreshing!

Never stop sharpening your saw! I'm excited to have a mastermind lunch today with a brilliant thought leader – a real 'mindset' guru. We view this meeting as an investment in the future of our businesses. Remember, investing in your business means investing in yourself because tactics and strategies are useless without the proper mindset.

"I like thinking big. If you're going to be thinking anything, you might as well think big." ~ Donald Trump

Add a zero to all of your goals. Want ten new clients next month? Go for 100 instead. If you fall woefully short, you'll still be miles ahead of hitting 100% of your smaller goal.

Chapter Twelve: Inspiration from the Trenches

In Chapter 2, we looked at examples of now-famous entrepreneurs who started their businesses in times of questionable economies. It's hard to imagine that those folks were ever where you are now because of their current fame and fortune. I'm here to tell you that there are plenty of unfamous entrepreneurs and small business owners who have decided to stop waiting and take the leap to launch their enterprises.

To help inspire and motivate you to "Stop Waiting for it to Get Easier," I thought the final section of this book should be some real-world stories of people who started their entrepreneurial journeys or launched aggressive growth campaigns within the last three years.

I've interviewed five such entrepreneurs, and I am including the transcripts of those interviews on the following pages, so you can read their stories *in their own words*. Here's what's coming up on the next several pages:

1. I interviewed a woman who started a small business part-time while being a stay-at-home mom who suddenly found herself divorced and needing to grow her business to support herself and her girls.
2. Next, I interviewed a man who has an outstanding corporate position, is the sole bread winner for his family, and decided to start a business part-time – with the goal of quitting his salaried position within one year!

3. Another highly inspirational story is that of an Iraqi war veteran who started a business less than a year ago and is already thriving big time!

4. Our next story is of a woman who had a career in the nonprofit sector, and when she became pregnant, she was determined to be a stay-at-home mom but needed a second income – and her home-based business was born.

5. Finally, you'll meet an entrepreneur who left a high-paying position as a sales rep to start a new business selling printing at a time when print businesses were closing their doors left and right.

These five entrepreneurs may not be famous (yet!), but each one is enjoying various levels of success running their own businesses and putting their efforts and creativity to work for profit rather than trading hours for dollars.

Melanie VanNuys: Part-time Start, Full-time Finish

Jim: Thank you for being a featured guest entrepreneur for this book, Melanie, I'm very excited to share your story with our readers. As you know, this book is written for those people who are perhaps unemployed or may be underemployed, are dreaming of starting a business, always had that entrepreneurial itch, or are perhaps waiting for the right time. I'm also aiming this information at new entrepreneurs, some of whom have already started either part-time or full-time and had some success but are yet unable to reach their dreams, their goals... whatever that might be, a six-figure business or beyond. Again, they are waiting even though they might have an idea or a new concept on how to get their business to the next level but are just being a little cautious. Maybe it's economy-driven or for other reasons, but I know some people are waiting for the right time to start a business. However, I know your story is going to resonate with a lot of readers because a lot of folks have gone through what you've been through in the last eighteen months to two years, so I'm excited to share your journey and your thoughts, including your fears... and this is what this book is all about.

In full disclosure to my readers, Melanie and I have been friends for almost five years. She is a private coaching member, a member of my mastermind group, and she's also a client, so I know her pretty well which is why I'm excited to share her story. So Melanie, how are you doing?

Melanie: I'm good, Jim and thank you for having me. I hope something I say will be able to help somebody else get started on their entrepreneurial journey.

Jim: Excellent. Can you take a brief moment and share a little bit about yourself personally, your family situation; maybe what your career was a couple of years ago, and your entrepreneurial journey. Let's cover the last eighteen months or so to where you are now, being an aggressive entrepreneur.

Melanie: I am 41, recently divorced. I have two children who are 16 and 18, two daughters who really are a big support to me. I started a business about three years ago... actually it's been just a little over three years now and things have changed since I first started it. As I said, recently divorced, so that's been a bit of a challenge, but I've made it and it's all coming together nicely, and I just keep plugging along, and that's where we are.

Jim: Melanie, I know when you started your business it was part-time because three years ago your kids were a little younger and your husband at the time was supporting the household – is that correct?

Melanie: Yes, that's true. I started in 2010, and I was a stay-at-home mom at the time. My kids were 13 and 15, and as you said, my husband was our main bread winner. He was employed full-time with a great job. We were really able to rely on his income to pay the bills and keep us afloat until I was up and running once I made the decision to go ahead and do this.

Jim: And so in the last ten to twelve months, obviously that situation has changed, and now you've found your part-time job really needs to be your full-time job as you support yourself and your girls.

Melanie: Absolutely. It has become my main source of income, and that does keep me motivated. It keeps me looking at new angles and trying new things, and as you said earlier, being aggressive and going after what I'm looking for.

Jim: Did you ever think of maybe going back to work and just getting the salary, direct deposit, benefits and all that? Or are you too gung-ho with the entrepreneurial mindset?

Melanie: Not a chance! I have always dreamed of having my own business for as long as I can remember. When I made the decision to do it, I knew then there was going to be no turning back. I was going to sink or swim, and I was going to do whatever I had to do to make sure it was successful. Again, not to keep beating the dead horse, with the changes in my personal life, that has become even more of a powerful driving force.

Jim: So it's fair to say, because you and I have worked together for a while, your goals initially, while they were darn nice goals, have changed dramatically because in this case, nothing is holding you back… either economy-wise or you're not necessarily waiting for the right time. In fact, the right time has been thrust upon you, I guess, for you to really take your business to the next level.

Melanie: It certainly has. Before I started this, I had read enough to know that the economy really doesn't have to play a factor in starting your business. There have been people who have started businesses in much worse conditions than what we're in right now, even when I started in 2010, and have become very successful. I don't let any of that kind of stuff hold me back.

Jim: That's so cool, Melanie. So tell our readers about your business.

Melanie: I am known as The Hometown Marketing Girl, and what I do is offer businesses help with learning how to use social media and mobile marketing to grow their businesses. I don't work typically with bigger stores or businesses; I do try to work with smaller businesses. I'm from a small town in rural Ohio, and small businesses are what keep us afloat around here, so I try to help them use tools that are at their disposal to level the playing field with their bigger competitors.

Jim: Now one of the things that I think is very interesting about your business and really tens of thousands of other businesses is that you are a home-based business, so you're able to run a very lean operation, right? And outside of maybe Internet, computer and things like that, realistically with the kind of services you're offering and the types of clients you're going after, you don't have a lot of expenses. Is that a fair statement?

Melanie: That is a very fair statement. In fact, some of my friends who realize now that I'm doing this and I'm working at it because I tell them, "Look, I can work anywhere I have wi-fi and cell service." And that's true. If I take trips with my girls, I tell them, "Listen I'm not taking the whole day off, I'm going to work for a few hours in the morning." I answer emails, make or return phone calls and then I'm done for the rest of the day. It's so simple and my overhead is next to nothing for me. It's wonderful.

Jim: And that's so true for a lot of business owners. Decades ago, even in the 70s and 80s, if you wanted to start a business, you had to rent an office even if you were going to do something similar to what you're doing now. Having a home-based office is not only a good way to start lean and mean, but it's very acceptable. I can remember times ten or fifteen years ago when you didn't necessarily want people to know you operated out of your home. They thought, "Well that's not really a real business." But it really is true today: people don't look down on home-based businesses.

Melanie: Right. The stigma is gone. It's a much more acceptable thing now. Women who are raising children, but still want to work, have the flexibility of working from home. With different changes coming in the future where businesses are going to have cut back on full-time work forces, a home-based business is going to be great because they can still work and support their family but not have to worry about commuting expenses, cut hours, or that type of thing.

Jim: Let's drill down a little bit and give readers a little glimpse into a home-based business. Literally, outside of your Internet and things like that, you don't meet clients in your home. Typically if you're going to meet with them, you'll go their office or maybe meet in a restaurant or some place similar. Is that right?

Melanie: That's correct. Typically I'll meet clients in their office or in a restaurant. And so after meeting a client, I'm back home again. Internet, cell service, a computer, I have an all-in-one fax/scanner/copier that makes sending documents back and forth simpler. That's it; there's nothing else.

Jim: So I think one of the big takeaways for people considering starting a home-based business, whether you're going through a personal situation like you are or even if you're not, you can start a business on a shoestring in many cases. You've got to order some business cards and maybe a few other things, but you don't need a big, fancy office; you don't need a big, fancy desk... you need your laptop. When I go on vacation or am going away, one of the first things I'll check out when we're looking to rent a place is the amenity list to see if there's high speed Internet. Stephanie's like, "Whatever." She's used to it... that's just how I go on vacation. I feel better when I can check in once in a while. But you know, you can actually operate a business anywhere, and you can certainly get started on a very small budget, so I think that's really a valuable point.

Melanie: If I can elaborate on just one more thing: Even if you can't afford Internet at home, there are plenty of coffee shops, restaurants, the library, or any place like that that offers free wi-fi. Grab your computer and sit there until you can make it to where you can eventually get Internet at home. There are plenty of ways around it, like you said, that you can literally start up on a shoestring.

Jim: I'm also reminded when you mentioned libraries that when I started my first business and I wanted to do some direct mail and even identify companies, I went down to our public library, into the reference department and jumped on a computer and accessed these databases and services similar to InfoUSA that are free at the public library. You can search out targeted lists and things like that, so that's another great tip.

Melanie: Absolutely.

Jim: You know what else, Melanie... and I just want to make clear that I am not an accountant and you should seek your own professional advice... but when you run a home-based business, you can write off cerain expenses related to your home office. If you're a Sub Chapter S Corporation, you can legitimately pay yourself rent from the corporation, and there are a number of things you can deduct such as a portion of utilities, a portion of the phone bill and things like that. There are some other tax advantages of having a home-based business. Again, I will say you will certainly want to consult with your accountant or attorney wherever applicable.

Melanie: You're absolutely right. I have a very simple business structure, so when I do my taxes each year, I meet with my accountant, and he goes over everything as far as those things you mentioned. But I can also mention that if you are buying your home, you can write off a portion of the mortgage interest you pay, your utilities, and all of those types of things. Also, mileage if you go and meet with clients at different places. Even if it's a few hundred miles a year, it's still a write off, so you want to make sure you take that into consideration, too. But again, as you said, I'm not an accountant either; I can only go by my personal experience. The perks are definitely there for being a home-based business.

Jim: Melanie, let's talk about mindset a little bit. Again, a lot of the message of this book is there is no perfect time, and again, I think the major timing of when you really needed to ramp up was kind of thrust upon you. But let's talk about the mindset of running your business: What gets you going, what gets you working harder, what gets you staying late, and making that extra sales call and things like that? What does it for you, Melanie?

Melanie: I'll tell you, again, it's the personal situation and this business being my sole income right now is a big, big motivator. My kids are another big motivating factor. I have one in college now so that's financially a big motivator for me. The other thing… and this is going to sound a little vain and I don't want it to come across that way… but I want to be able to say, "I did it. I made it, through the challenges, through the ups and downs, through everything else, I did it." I want to be able to say to my girls, "You can do it too, whatever you put your mind to. Outside factors don't have to determine what you can or can't do, it just takes a little bit of hard work." There are days that I work until 8 or 9 at night, which are rare, but if I do it's worth it in the end if I can pull that off.

Jim: I learned 12 years ago that life can be short, so you never want to have any regrets, so I believe it's worth taking the shot. A very big motivator for me in writing this book is that people wait and wait and wait, and the next thing you know, it is too late, so I think there is no better time than right now to chase your dream, and if you've got the entrepreneurial itch by all means you should scratch it. Do you have one or two role models that have influenced your decision to become an entrepreneur?

Melanie: I do. I'm going to tell you thanks to you, Jim, and our friendship and work affiliation, and I know you're going to say one or two, but I have to throw this in there: As I grew with you and worked with you and you encouraged me to join that first mastermind group if you remember, I was scared to death and almost hung up the phone on that first call because I was near tears. But I found out they were all right there with me, and it was okay. There were books that I read in the beginning. I turned to you as a coach and a mentor and without a doubt you have definitely been a big role model for me and my business. Another person that I consider a role model, again thanks to you, is Carrie Wilkerson. I learned about her through you and on a trip home from Florida one year I read her book *The Barefoot Executive* from cover to cover, and that changed my whole outlook. I know you said two but I'm adding one more: recently I was able to listen to an interview you did with Dave Frees, and it completely changed my life professionally and personally. So I have to say those are the three who have had the biggest impact on me.

Jim: Well, thank you Melanie, and I think that everyone needs to have someone in their corner pushing them, holding them accountable. In fact, the more success you have, you should never *not* have a coach or shouldn't *not* become part of a mastermind group. As the owner of our businesses, there's nobody higher than us, right? So if there's something that's not getting done, we have no one to hold us accountable, and that's why it's a good idea to have a coach. So let's talk about that quickly – talk about investing in your future. I always talk about investing in your future growth and future profitability. I remember when you talked to me about joining the mastermind and joining my coaching program, it was a big stretch for you. What caused you to make that decision?

Melanie: You're right. Even though at the time I joined that first mastermind group I was still married and still had my husband's income and support, I was still making an investment in my business. That didn't come out of our personal money; that came out of what I had to come up with as far as business money, so it was a stretch financially for me in the beginning, but I did it. I'm not going to lie: I was scared to death, but I'm so glad I did it. I knew there were other people out there who were further along than I was on the path and who would absolutely give me the information and guidance that I needed, even if it was just a "hey, you know, this is a good idea" or "no, don't do that, stay away from that… you don't want to go that way." In other words, not telling me what I wanted to hear. If I shared good ideas, I got "yes"; if it was a bad idea, you all either led me in another direction or just said to completely forget it. And the other thing was that I liked the idea of the accountability behind a mastermind group. There is no "oh yeah, I'll do that" and then it falls by the wayside. Every month when we meet, you're held accountable: "Did you do that? How did it work? If you didn't do it, why not?" I really like that accountability part of it, so those things ultimately led me to say, "Okay, let's do this."

Jim: Another important point that you made about being in a mastermind group: Some people think it's all about getting ideas and say, "Well I don't need ideas; I'm running with it." Being in a mastermind group and being with other entrepreneurs, there's permission there for someone to say "No, you're going the wrong way; go this way." So it actually saves you some pain. Pain teaches us lessons, but if you can avoid some pain because somebody has been there and done that, that's a good thing. Melanie, what are three books that you've read that you would suggest to somebody who is considering starting a business or maybe they have a business and are trying to get to the next level.

Melanie: Again, you kept me to three, but I'm going to go with the three that were the most influential when I was first starting out. Any of your readers will know this book and you have mentioned it many times over the years: *Think and Grow Rich*. This is a big one, and anyone who is ready to start a business or has started should read this without a doubt. Another one that I mentioned earlier was Carrie Wilkerson's *The Barefoot Executive*. That was a great book that helped get me in the right mindset from a woman's point of view. Another one that really caught me was *The One Minute Millionaire*, and it really showed me that there was more to building wealth than just making money. So that was really a good book for me. Not to mention, I've read all of your books, and between your books and coaching, they've all helped influence me.

Jim: Now that you're up and running, Melanie, would you say it's harder than your thought, easier than you thought, or completely different than you thought it would be?

Melanie: I think probably it's more different than I thought it would be. A lot of us start a business thinking it's going to lead us into this glamorous lifestyle, and we can sit on the beach all day and eat bon bons while the money just pours in. Owning a business can definitely lead to a very comfortable life, but not without doing the work. So it's definitely different – not easier or harder. My day-to-day stuff is pretty much second nature now, but if there is one area that's a challenge, it is staying motivated and focused on those nice days where you would much rather be outside doing something else. If something happens that I can't sit in that office for another second, I'll grab the laptop and go on my deck or to the park and do some writing.

Jim: Last question: If you have one piece of advice to say to the readers of this book who are either starting a business or those who own a business but are sitting on the sidelines waiting for it to get easier before they aggressively jump in or aggressively market their current business, what would you say?

Melanie: I would say stop waiting and get busy. There's no better time than right now to either start a business or build a business that can ultimately lead to the life of your dreams. There's no point in waiting until it gets easier. What are you going to be doing while you're waiting for that perfect time or that perfect moment? The time is going to pass anyway, so you might as well go for it now. One thing I have to say is I've learned more looking in the rearview mirror than I ever have looking out over the hood, so don't waste another minute and risk a lifetime of "what if."

Jim: I think we'll close on the title of my fourth book *It is OK to be Scared But Never Give Up*. Melanie how can people learn more about you or connect with you? What's your website address?

Melanie: You can reach me at www.hometownmarketinggirl.com and from there you can find me on Facebook, Twitter or contact me via email.

Jim: Awesome thank you so much for being a part of this book, Melanie, I greatly appreciate it.

Melanie: Thank you, Jim.

Nile Nickel: Corporate Success to Entrepreneurial Boom in One Year

Jim: Nile, thank you for being a featured guest entrepreneur for this book. I'm really excited to share you with our readers. I know your story is going to resonate with a lot of readers because you had a career at the time and have had a pretty successful career for a long time, but you're sort of starting your entrepreneurial journey part-time but still working a lot of hours. Frankly what impresses me about you, Nile, is that you're moving full steam ahead with a new business, ramping up as quickly as possible, so you can actually make your entrepreneurial venture your full-time deal.

I want to say to our readers that Nile and I have known each other, have been friends, for probably almost five years, and Nile is also a member of my coaching program, so I know him really well. I know his story will resonate with you.

So Nile, how are you doing today?

Nile: Doing wonderful, Jim and thanks for the time and the interview today.

Jim: My pleasure. Can you take a moment and share a little about who you are personally, maybe your family, so people can understand the dynamic and briefly explain your career to whatever degree you're comfortable, and then we'll talk about your new entrepreneurial journey.

Nile: Sure. I am a 55-year-old gentleman starting another business. I say another business because I've started a number of them. But there are a couple of things that have prompted me to start this business. Two of those are that I had gotten remarried to a wonderful woman about ten years ago, and she decided that she wanted to have children; she's younger than I am. I was excited about that possibility. So I have my wife, Rosemary, and we have two beautiful children. We didn't wait very long, and now I've got a big family that I'm supporting all over again as opposed to planning my retirement. While I might have been able to rest on my laurels a bit, I can't do that any longer. I started looking at this current business I was in and I didn't see, for a number of reasons that we won't necessarily get into, where it was going to reach the financial goals that I needed to live, nor did I see that it was really being very rewarding to me. So I started looking at what options I had.

Jim: Nile, you mentioned that you had started a number of businesses in the past, were they always, for lack of a better description, part-time businesses while you had a salaried position, or did you ever own a business and have that be your sole source of income?

Nile: No, actually I started out... I say I started out – I had a number of jobs when I was fairly young. I started working almost full-time at about age 12, seriously. So I'd had a number of jobs, and my father had a grocery store. I ended up running the grocery store for him at times. My mother had a laundromat, and I ran it for about a year by myself... all before I was legally able to drive. I was convinced at a young age I knew all about business, everything I needed to know, and I knew I could just do it. So I started a business when I was 16. Unfortunately, I didn't know about marketing, I didn't know about planning, I didn't know about budgeting or really much about selling – at least not yet anyway. What I didn't know was that I was ignorantly confident. I knew that I could make it because I'd done all these other things. That was my first venture into the entrepreneurial lifestyle.

Jim: It's fair to say that you have entrepreneurship in your genes, so it's really not a big surprise that you've been dabbling since you were 12 years old in the entrepreneurial world.

Nile: After a bit of time, I started that when I was 16 out of necessity. I couldn't get a full-time job anywhere, and I was married at 16 and I also had a child at 16. I had a family to support, so it was a necessity; I had to do it. So I started out that way. When I got a little bit older – the ripe old age of 19 – I got a full-time job that I thought was just great. I didn't have to worry about all this other stuff and managing my business and doing x and y and z, and I worked in the corporate world for a while, up to a big corporate experience with Rockwell International. We used to say we made everything from the Space Shuttle to electric drills. So I've been on both sides of the fence, but I have to say it's a whole lot more fun and more rewarding in the entrepreneurial world than it is in the big corporate world.

Jim: Working for profits instead of a paycheck as we say.

Nile: Yeah – and one of the things that I figured out later than I would have liked to figure out was if you're working for somebody else, you're going to be making at least two to three times what they're paying you... at least, more likely five to ten times what they're paying you. You're really earning your keep right now or they wouldn't be keeping you. Once you turn that into the entrepreneurial mindset and you start asking, "How can I turn this into something I can do for myself," it's where you start thinking differently about it.

Jim: I really think that people need a little bit of a push because there is no perfect time to start a business. And as you've shared, you have a second family now. You've got dreams and goals, and there's going to be college coming up and all kinds of things. So I'm guessing if I were to name timing, the economy, or any other external factors that are really driving and motivating you, it really is to provide for your family, and you know from your past entrepreneurial experience, you can do that in a better way owning your own successful business – is that fair?

Nile: That's very fair. I know that if you think about it very much, the economy right now isn't great and certainly if I were looking at that, there's no way that I could do that. I know that in the core business that I operate in right now, it's busy, it's full. As a matter of fact, I would have thought it would be slowing down; it's growing… go figure. So you might look at all those things and say it's really not the time to do that. The only problem is there is no time except right now. If you don't do it now, you never will. Whether it's taking the first step and it's a minor step or it's jumping in with both feet, if you don't take that first step, you're never going to get there.

Jim: One of the things I'm so admiring about you in starting this journey is I know that you do have a great job right now, but you're starting this new business. Part of the new business is based on things and skills that you've learned over the last several years, but certainly more in the last three to four years, your skills have been really honed and developed, and you're actually carving out a niche for yourself in the world of teaching people how to use LinkedIn.

Nile: Yeah, LinkedIn and social media. I've been in social media my entire life. The first venture that I ventured into that I mentioned earlier was that I opened up a CB business. I sold, serviced and installed citizen band radios when that craze was going on, back before most people will know that means in this book probably. So I've always been in that world, but you're right, I started to use LinkedIn in my core business probably about five or six years ago, and I just started to get phenomenal results. And as I started to get those results, in 2012 I had a "tick mark" thing and for everybody who asked me to help them I added a "tick" and when the "tick" got to number 50, I said, "Okay, it's time that I need to do something different with this rather than just helping people for thanks and appreciation." And that's what really caused me to start down this journey. I knew that I wanted to do something else; I just didn't know what that something else was going to be.

Jim: You know what's interesting is in a previous chapter I talk about keeping your eyes opening and be listening for opportunities because friends, clients – if you already have a business – and people that you are interacting with are always telling you about a pain they have or a need they have, and when they get to know you have a certain skill, they always reach out to you. I think human nature in a lot of cases says "Well let me help my friend" or "Just let me help this person." But in reality, like you said, you get to a certain point where you say, "Wow there could really be a business here," and so there's a lesson there. The other lesson I've written about is that you can generate profit when you solve enough pain for people. And pain is not necessarily a bad thing. For example, if you get a stone on your windshield or if some kind of thug breaks your windshield, that's a pain you have. If that never happened, there would be no windshield repair businesses. If you didn't have bugs coming into your house once in a while, there would be no need for exterminators. Pain is not always profiting from other people's agony, but in a lot of cases most businesses are providing a service that is needed, and it's solving somebody's pain. One of the things that is so exciting about your business in teaching people about LinkedIn strategies, how to grow their businesses, how to drive traffic and all the things that you're doing is you are actually solving pain because people need to connect with people whether they're an employee or an entrepreneur trying to grow their business, so you are actually helping people who have a need.

Nile: You know it came out of my own testing, but I realized in my core business that I deal with, it's a very niche business, and it was very, very hard identifying decision makers in my business, and that's why I started using LinkedIn personally. I found some ways in a very niche business to have people raise their hand, come forward and say,"I'm interested in doing business with you" which is the ideal situation. But you mentioned something else, and I mentioned that I'd worked for my father in his grocery store and I remember way back when all my friends would come in, and

I'd want to give them discounts on everything. One day he pulled me aside and said, "You know your enemies don't come buy from you." So ideally, your friends are going to be the ones doing business with you all the time, and if you give them discounts all the time, you're never going to be in business very long. That was a little bit of a lesson that came out of last year as well. Like I said, by the time I got to number 50, it was like a sledgehammer pounding me over the head rather than a little tap or whisper in my ear.

Jim: Nile, can you talk about the fear factor? When it comes to pulling the trigger to either start the business or launch a new venture, how do you overcome the fear factor that holds so many people dead in their tracks?

Nile: Well I don't know that we ever get over that. As I said, I've done a number of businesses. This one is nothing new as far as that goes. But I can tell you that I probably had more angst over this business than I did any business in the past. And maybe it's because the stakes were higher or that I had a bigger family and a younger family. One of the things that I did was said, "Okay, what am I afraid of first off?" What I was afraid of was that I was going to start down this path, we're going to jump into it and this is going to be our income at some point in time, and it may not be the same income. It may be less. It may cause me to lose my current income. So I sat the family down and we talked through all of those issues, and I explained to them what my fears were. Not only did they sort of alleviate those fears, but I got buy-in from the family. Because the other thing I knew was it was going to take a lot of time and effort, and dad might not be in the house as much as dad usually was. So I wanted to make sure we were all on board with this, and that's one of the best things I did because in addition to getting them on board and helping and supporting me, they also keep me on track. If they see me getting down and depressed about something, they become, literally from my seven-year-old little girl up to my wife, the biggest cheerleaders that I could have.

Jim: That's so awesome. I had the same situation, and it is really cool when they cheer you on. Quite frankly, I went through a situation when I was unemployed. But when my kids were teenagers, they learned the value of going out and earning money for what they wanted. Dad was no longer standing at the door Friday night saying, "Oh here's money for bowling; here's money for movies." If they wanted anything, they had to go earn it, and I look back on that as kind of a blessing in our life. So, wrapping up here, do you have two or three books that have really been an influence and helped you kind of start or build your business or helped you with the mindset?

Nile: I had to laugh; you sent me that question and asked it and I had to laugh. Because if I was to name two or three books that are my favorite, my wife would say we could probably clear out two rooms of the house that are full of books. I do have a couple that are high on my list, but I probably read anywhere five to ten books a month, sometimes more than that. It's hard to identify, but the two that come to mind initially are *Think and Grow Rich* which, while it's an old book, every time I re-read it – and I don't know how many times I've read it – I get something different from it. One is a newer book, and I know that you're in love with this book as well, *The Slight Edge*. Then I said, "Gosh, if I had to pick one other one, it's going to be some sort of nonfiction business book that's related to sales, marketing or business. And again, I read so many really it's hard to pick one.

Jim: But actually built into your answer is a very big nugget for everyone reading this book – you've got to read constantly. That is the way we keep learning and educating ourselves, so that's a great answer in and of itself. Now that you're up and running and growing this new business, would you say it's harder than you thought, easier than you thought or just completely different than you thought?

Nile: I don't think it's harder or easier. I think some things are easier, some things are a lot harder, but one thing you can 100%

accurately predict is it's always going to be different. It's always different than we think it's going to be or imagine it's going to be.

Jim: If you had one piece of advice, Nile, to say to the readers of this book who are either considering starting a business or those who own a business now but maybe haven't achieved anywhere near their dreams or their goals and in both cases, they're kind of sitting on the sidelines waiting before they jump in, what would you say to those people?

Nile: This might sound a little bit crazy, but I would say do something even if it's wrong. That might sound funny, but we just talked about how it's going to be different than you imagine it's going to be. You're going to learn from that. By the way, the people that tend to be the most successful in any of their businesses have a number of failures under their belt. So if you can just get in your head "this could fail, but I'll learn a valuable lesson in this business, it makes me stronger and better prepared to do it the next time," that's fine. You get up to bat playing baseball or softball, whatever it may be, and just because you swing and miss you've got strike one, you swing and miss again and you've got strike two. You've still got another ball coming at you. But even if you strike out, you're going to be up to bat again. Don't be worried about that process.

Jim: Nile, what's a website where people can learn more about you and what you're doing?

Nile: The website for the business that I'm most excited about right now is the one we talked about, my new business is www.linkedinfocus.com. I'd love you to come there, and if your readers come to that site, there's also a free gift on there where they can start applying some LinkedIn strategies and get some results from it immediately.

Jim: Awesome. Nile, thank you very much, I really appreciate your time and your inspiration for the readers of this book – thank you!

Nile: Thanks, Jim.

John Lee Dumas: Stoking Entrepreneurial Passion and Success

Jim: Hey John Lee, thank you for being one of the featured guest entrepreneurs for the book. I'm really excited to share your journey as well as what your thoughts are, including any fears you had or have, or what gets you excited. I know your story is going to hit home with readers because you started your business right about a year ago, and you've had some pretty doggone good success – proving the point and the message that now is the time for readers of this book to get into action.

John: Jim, it's great to be here and thank you for this opportunity.

Jim: My pleasure. Hey, what were you doing when you decided to become an entrepreneur?

John: I was a commercial real estate broker, I joined one of those traditional firms, I was on partnership track, and I was just settled in for the long haul. It was going to be a tough few years because the market was bad, but I had a great career ahead of me if I just stuck with it. But there was just no passion, no excitement for me. When deals did happen, I wasn't giving anyone high fives because it was just like "Eh, okay... let's move on to the next thing." I always wanted that passion, I wanted it. So that's what I was doing before I launched my first real passion in life "Entrepreneur on Fire."

Jim: Were you nervous? Full of energy and courage? Convinced you'd be a success or kind of all of the above or none of the above?

John: I was full of energy, full of enthusiasm; chock full of fear, terror, panic, all of the above.

Jim: That's the way we roll isn't it?

John: That's how we roll.

Jim: Did you quit your job? Did you start part-time or did you just say sayonara and I'm going to start Entrepreneur on Fire?

John: I went cold turkey, Jim, I really did. It was one of those situations that I was able to do so. I don't recommend it to everybody because some people just do have those monthly commitments that are stacked up, and you should start with one toe at a time to ease yourself into the entrepreneurial waters. But for me, I just cannonballed in. I did have a runway, not the longest runway in the world, but I did have some prior successes in my ventures which gave me that runway, so I was very fortunate to be in that situation. But again, I would say, going either way is the right way to do it, whatever works best for you. But I went straight cold turkey.

Jim: I guess for those people who are just meeting you for the first time, you're single, so you didn't have a wife, mortgage, kids, and all that stuff that goes with it.

John: My overhead was pretty low.

Jim: So what was or what is the biggest reason or motivation for launching Entrepreneur on Fire?

John: I saw a void that needed to be filled. I really did because it was something that I loved, which were podcasts. There was no show coming out with the kind of consistency and quantity that I needed as somebody who drove to work every single day, somebody who went to the gym five times a week and was looking to consume great content at those times in my life. But podcasting was out there, and there were great hosts doing great things, but I knew that I wanted to be that person who was able to step into that void that I saw and create a seven-day-a-week podcast and interview today's most inspiring and successful entrepreneurs. I knew that I wanted it, and I knew there were other people out there like me who were commuting to work by themselves every single day. In fact, in the US, there are 90 million of them, and I knew there were people who were going to the gym and on the treadmill who were trying to consume high-quality content that was going to improve them as a business mind. So that's exactly why I created

Entrepreneur on Fire... because it was a niche and a void that I saw was out there, and I sought out to fill it.

Jim: You know the great thing about your story, John Lee, is that you saw a need and filled it which is how most successful businesses start. You know, people become creatures of habit. We go to the same dry cleaner, we drink the same beer for the most part or whatever it is, so it's hard to necessarily break habits. If someone likes a particular podcast, it's really smart, because like you said: people go to the gym every day, they commute every day, and there's another show coming next week. so you're forced to have this huge rotation. But for you serving it up every day, they just get hooked, and that's probably to a large degree why your numbers have grown so dramatically.

John: I would definitely agree to that because I'm a huge believer in habits. We are creatures of habits, and a lot of my listeners wake up and shower, they pour a cup of coffee, they download Entrepreneur on Fire, and then they take off to work. That's become a daily ingrained habit. If it was only once a week, then it wouldn't become a habit for them, they would maybe do it one time and then skip a couple of weeks and then remember and go back to it. But this way, I can become part of their everyday lives and for me on the other end of the spectrum as the host, I'm getting to meet incredible entrepreneurs on a very high-quantity level. Jim, you're a great example of somebody that I've met and there have been others like Gary Vaynerchuk, Seth Godin who I've interviewed on my show because I do such high quantity... where if I was only doing once a week, I would only be talking to 50 amazing entrepreneurs a year instead of 365, and you talk about numbers, you're actually right. We just crossed our 300th episode of Entrepreneur on Fire. Last month, we had 308,000 unique downloads, and now we're going to be featured on the iTunes Home Page for the dates of August 20-August 27 in celebration of our 300th episode, and it's all because of this consistency, this quantity and just sticking to that plan.

Jim: That is so cool, congratulations. So this book is really a lot about mindset, and I'm really trying to inspire people to take the entrepreneurial plunge. So when you decided to do this, did you even consider the timing, the economy, any external factors or did you just say, "This is a great idea, let's go"?

John: Heck no. There are always reasons to complain and whine and give excuses. The economy is never perfect. Just like I hear over and over again, there's never a perfect time to have a baby, you just have to go and have one. This is the exact same thing. There is never a perfect time to become an entrepreneur, you just have to go out and do it and actually take that action. And that is exactly what I did. I just had the "aha" moment and that light bulb went off. The next step that I took, Jim, was critical... and this one thing that I love to share with Entrepreneur on Fire listeners... is that I went out and invested in myself immediately. I reached out to an industry leader in my niche – Jamie Tardy of The Eventual Millionaire. She had been a very successful podcaster for a number of years. I reached out to her and asked her to coach and mentor me, and she agreed. It wasn't cheap, Jim, it cost $1000 a month, and I signed on for a three-month period. But guess what? It was of incredible value. She pressed the fast forward button for me. She introduced me to the movers and shakers in the industry. She helped my mindset. She allowed me to get over certain hurdles that could have held me back, all because I was willing to invest in myself and I sought out an industry leader. So I think those are some great takeaways for the readers.

Jim: Absolutely and I especially like the way you said invest – you didn't say you went out and bought a coach or paid for training – you *invested* in your future success. So in that three-month period, looking back on that now John Lee, how much do you think that accelerated you? In other words, you went all the way around the Monopoly board, you didn't just get to the first railroad. That three-month period took you all the way around and passed "Go" probably.

John: Great analogy. The fast forward button that I pressed saved me six months if not an entire business because so many people end up getting caught up on the little things and incorrect mindset, and then they end up giving up and walking away. That very well could have happened to me, but with Jamie guiding me, showing me her shining example of success, I was able to keep my confidence level up, which is so critical in those beginning stages.

Jim: Everybody talks about having a safety net or a Plan B. I think my mindset and I'm guessing yours is the same is to avoid that. I've heard this expression, "Cut the rope," and there is no choice – you have to go. I've shared with you that my first year in business was revenue-free, and I just did not give up. Imagine if I had given up the seventh month, eighth month, ninth month, tenth month, eleventh month – this isn't working. Little did I know there were several new clients ready to come on board. You didn't have a safety net either, I'm guessing?

John: Absolutely not.

Jim: Now I know that you invested in a mentor. Did you have any role models in your life as far as the gene pool… as far as helping you become an entrepreneur?

John: I definitely grew up in a very entrepreneurial family. My father was a lawyer, so that doesn't strike you particularly as an entrepreneur per se, but when he was 29 years old, I had just been born, so here he is a 29-year-old guy, he had just gotten out of the Army, and he hung his own shingle and started his own business. So he had to do everything. He was the lawyer, he was the landlord, he was the business owner, everything that was involved with running a business… he was running his own business. And throughout his career, he shifted and pivoted many times as the economy shifted and pivoted. Whether that be real estate or worker's compensation or social security benefits, whatever that may be or whatever the rising tide, he was able to pivot because he was an entrepreneur, because he was controlling the ship, he had his hands on the rudder. That was always a very good mentor for me growing up, realizing that those people who took control and had the reigns of their business were really able to put themselves in much more fruitful situations.

Jim: That's awesome. One of the things I envisioned when writing this book, John Lee, is that people are standing at the precipice of pulling the trigger – "I want to do it," but they're probably stuck in the new cycle. So I'm really hoping this is the thing that kicks them in the rear end and gets them to take action. Can you talk a little bit about the fear factor when it comes down to pulling the trigger to start a business or pull the trigger to get a new venture going, if they have a couple of wheels in the soft shoulder. Did you experience the fear? How did you overcome the fear?

John: So the fear is present, it's going to be there for every single person, it's an innate fear. We are all born with it, we are all human beings and that fear is a survival technique that we all have. It's always going to be there for every single person no matter what you do. President Obama wakes up every morning with a slight bit of fear in his gut because he's human, because that's an innate fear that we all need to overcome as entrepreneurs and really just as human beings in general. For me, my biggest thing that I always recommend is that this is where you need to find a mastermind. This is where you need to find a group of like-minded entrepreneurs who are all experiencing this fear, who are able and willing to talk about it and share the fear and share the successes and to motivate and encourage each other, to give each other feedback when necessary. For me with Entrepreneur on Fire, I saw how needed something like this was for my listeners, my massive audience was telling me over and over again that they are feeling this fear and had no community to support them. So Jim that's when I launched a membership mastermind for Entrepreneur on Fire – Fire Nation Elite. This is a community for entrepreneurs that want to be part of a tribe of like-minded entrepreneurs who are going to support each other, motivate each other, give each other criticism when it's needed, but most importantly, be committed to each other's success. So as we're speaking right now Jim, there are 82 members of Fire Nation. We're growing very slowly and very organically every single day because I'm committed to talking to each and every applicant one-on-one before offering them a spot because I want it to be filled with the right people. So that would be what I would say to your readers: find your mastermind, find your community and if you can't find one, create one. Be the leader that you want. I was able to create Fire Nation Elite and form it into the ways that I most wanted a membership mastermind to be all about. So the readers can do that as well if they can't find one that they think is right for them.

Jim: It's such a powerful thing and I love what you're doing with Fire Nation Elite. When I joined my first mastermind it was in 2006, the investment was $400 a month and it might as well been $4000 or $40,000 because I really wasn't generating that kind of extra cash at the time. But I knew that by being connected to other entrepreneurs, being held accountable, getting ideas and things like that, I knew that $400 investment would be toward new profits for the business, and about six or eight months later, it was easy for me to write that check. That's one area of the business that I always tell people to put the cart before the horse because in the end you're really going to go so much faster by being in a mastermind. So what are three books that you would recommend reading? What are some of the ones you've read multiple times?

John: I think you might have been the actual guest I had on Entrepreneur on Fire that put me on to one of these three books. I'm not positive about that, but one book that I've loved for the longest time was Darren Hardy's *The Compound Effect* and that's one that I'll recommend right here. The one that I hadn't heard of that actually inspired *The Compound Effect* was *The Slight Edge* by Jeff Olsen.

Jim: Yes, I was the one that recommended *The Slight Edge*.

John: I thought that was you – so I went and read that book immediately and was really blown away by its amazing message and everything that was going on within that book. Those would be two of the three, and for my third one, I'm going a little further back in time than either one of those two books because this one is something that I actually just found out about two months ago. I got this audio book and it blew me away because we all know Napoleon Hill and we all know *Think and Grow Rich,* and that's not the book I'm recommending although that's a great book. He also wrote a book around the same time back in the 1930s called *Outwitting the Devil*, and that book was not released until 2011. It was held in the vault for 70+ years, and in 2011 was released by the Napoleon Hill Foundation, and now it's available both in the book and in the audio version, and wow is it awesome.

Jim: It is a great book. So John I've got two more questions for you. Now that you're up and running, and really enjoying some great and well-deserved success, John Lee, would you say it's harder than you thought, easier than you thought or possibly completely different than you thought?

John: I'd say it's a lot easier than I thought, and I'd say it goes back to *The Slight Edge* principles where if you do put in the time and you do put in the hard and consistent work which I have done from day one and continue to do so to the present day, all of that snowball effect that's been happening all of these months continues to go. So then, you get to this point, Jim, where the momentum starts to take control, the machine that you've created is starting to move on its own and that's what I'm seeing with Entrepreneur on Fire. When I wake up in the morning, I've seen that there's been 5000 more downloads over the night on my podcast. There have been book purchases, there've been affiliate sales, there've been more people joining Fire Nation Elite or at least requesting to have a 15-minute chat with me for it, so it's this consistent ball of momentum that is just continuing to grow with steam and making everything that I do easier.

Jim: Momentum is a great thing. Momentum, once you get it going is great. I'm at the mindset now where I could accelerate a little bit but I don't want to because I don't want the car to start coasting. Momentum is such a great thing because it's really like you said earlier, a snowball getting bigger and I don't want to put anything in the way right now.

John: Yes.

Jim: Final question: If you had one piece of advice to say to the readers of this book who are currently right now either considering starting a business or maybe they own a business and haven't hit six figures yet or whatever their personal goals are and are basically sitting, waiting for it to get easier before they aggressively take the plunge, what would you say?

John: I would honestly say just start. And that doesn't mean just go the cannonball route like I did. It means start wading in if that's a better method for you. Wake up 15 minutes earlier, go to bed 15 minutes later every single day. Use those 30 minutes for nothing else but to further your education in the field that you're passionate about and that is also a viable business. In six months, Jim, with *The Slight Edge* method applied, everybody will be amazed at how far they've come and the positions they've put themselves in to really take that plunge full-time.

Jim: That's awesome. Well John Lee you're a good friend, you're one heck of a professional, and I highly recommend to everyone reading this book to make listening to John's podcast part of your daily routine. John, how can people connect with you and learn more about you and your awesome Entrepreneur on Fire brand?

John: Well thanks for that, Jim. Entrepreneur is not an easy word to spell so I made it easier – www.eofire.com will get you to my home base, and that's where you can find out anything you like.

Jim: That's awesome. John, thank you so much for being part of this book. I appreciate it.

Jessica Rhodes: Stay-at-Home Success

Jim: Jessica, thank you for being one of my featured guest entrepreneurs. I am excited to share your story with our readers.

There's a growing number of women who have or have had careers but now want to be stay-at-home moms, but in a lot of cases, they can't afford to live on just the husband's income, so I think your story is going to resonate – how you got started, your home-based business and things like that so thank you so much for being part of the book.

Jessica: Well thank you for asking me. I'm really excited to share my story because as you said I think it will resonate with a lot of women, so thank you for interviewing me.

Jim: In full disclosure to our readers, Jessica works for me – I am coaching her in her new business and even more important and exciting than that, Jessica is my daughter and mom to my most awesome grandson, Nathan! Jessica, do take a moment and share a little bit of your back story and what brought you to this point today.

Jessica: I'll just give you a really short summary of my life over the past six or seven years. I went to college in Philadelphia at Temple University and met my husband when I was 19 years old, and he moved up to Rhode Island not even a month after we started dating, so we were in long distance relationship while I was in college until I knew I was going to be moving up here to Rhode Island to be with him. Luckily, the job I had at a nonprofit in Philadelphia also had an office there, so I was actually working for this nonprofit for about six years. We got married in October 2011, and last summer, about a year ago, we decided that we wanted to start a family, and I always knew I wanted to be a stay-at-home mom. My mom was a stay-at-home mom, and that was a really important part of my childhood and my siblings' childhood to have our mom there with us. So I knew I wanted to be at home with my child. I didn't know how it was going to happen financially, but I was really strong about that opinion, and I just knew I was going to make it happen. So then my dad... you... told me about starting a business as a virtual assistant, and you really pushed me to do it, and I'm so glad that you did because it's really opened up so many

143

opportunities. I create my own schedule, I have the ability to grow my income or make it smaller if I need to work a little bit less and be with my son more. So it's really just that drive to be at home with my son that ultimately got me to this place in my life.

Jim: So you were working when you decided to be an entrepreneur, but the driving force that led you to the entrepreneurial world was that you wanted to be, first and foremost, stay-at-home mom to Nathan.

Jessica: Correct. I was working when I decided to be an entrepreneur, but I decided to be a mom before that. So by the book, I probably wasn't doing things as smart as I could have done them because I got pregnant before I got the idea of what I was going to do to have an income when I was a mom. But I just needed that urgency; I need there to be a hard and fast deadline when I need to figure something out. That's why we went to start a family before I knew what was going to happen. I just needed that urgency in my life.

Jim: Which is a classic sign of entrepreneurship: We all dive in before we know where we're actually going to land. So let me ask you, were you nervous, full of energy and courage, or have you always been convinced you would be a success, or kind of all of the above?

Jessica: The short answer is all of the above, but I want to say a little bit about what I did in my last job. I was in a fundraising position and was literally door-to-door asking for money – that's how I made a living, and it's crazy that that's what I did, but it taught me so many skills. The one skill that I brought with me was the ability to obtain support. When you look somebody in the eye and ask them for money for fundraising or you ask them to become a customer, you really have to assume that they're going to say yes, and you have to assume that it's going to work out. That is honestly the one skill that keeps me going. I assume I'm going to be a success. I assume that I'm going to be making over six figures one day. I assume that this is all going to go well and that's what keeps me going. I just have this dangerous optimism, and I think sometimes that's scary for my husband. Maybe we are still tight on money for me to be so positive and optimistic – it makes him a little nervous, but that's what I need to have in my mind and keep growing and be successful. I just assume I'm going to make it and that's that.

Jim: You mentioned you got pregnant and you were still working. I remember when we were talking about becoming a virtual assistant and making a home-based business that you were still working and pregnant, and it was kind of getting near the end of the pregnancy, but you actually started your business part-time, nights and weekends, which I think is important, so people don't think, "Okay, stop one, start the other... how do I get it going, so I don't get that lull where nothing is happening?" So talk about how you initially pulled the trigger and got started.

Jessica: The transition started Thanksgiving this past year when I was at your house. That's when we really got the plan going, ordered a new laptop, so I could really have that resource to be able to work at home at nights and in the mornings. For the last three or four months of the pregnancy, I was getting up early in the morning, doing an hour or two of work before I went to the office. I would come home and work at night and work on the weekends. I did that for several months for a couple of reasons. I wanted to know what skills I was best at, so before I was actually a full-time entrepreneur, I wanted to know what skills I could offer to other clients other than you. So having three or four months just having a lot of different things for your business as a VA gave me that time to figure out what I was going to offer. So ultimately, now I have niched my business down to where I just have a couple of services that I specialize in. But working part-time and having my full-time job to go to during the day allowed me to get my feet wet in a lot of different areas.

Jim: I think the big lesson here is that you and I, working as your coach, weren't 100% sure where you were going to go and what you were going to do and what your strengths would be, but we did get you started doing some client services work, some behind the scenes admin stuff, just to get you used to that working-from-home mode where you're not actually going into the office, but I think what's going to resonate with so many readers is that you made the commitment that even though you were working full-time and starting to lose some of your waking hours, you did make the commitment for two, three or four months to get up a little early, stay up a little later and maybe work a little on the weekends to start honing your craft, so you could hit the ground running.

Jessica: I really want to emphasize that a lot of people think "I couldn't possibly get up earlier. I have to go to bed at a certain time," and it's amazing what you can get your body to do if you put your mind to it. I mean, up until I gave birth to my son, I was working extremely long hours – I actually sent an email from my iPhone when I was in labor at the hospital to tie up loose ends for work. It takes an insane amount of urgency, but you can do it. I started working again and picking up my work two weeks after my son was born, and people thought I was insane. But I could do it, it wasn't hurting me at all. I was on the couch with my laptop, so you really just have to want to do it and have the drive and just make it happen.

Jim: You know, a good friend of mine, Henry Evans, wrote a book called *The Hour a Day Entrepreneur.* Henry called himself a "corporate schmuck" working the whole grind, but when he wanted to start his own business, he would basically come home from work, have dinner with his wife and two girls, spend a little time with them and then when they went to bed, he would spend at least an hour in the evening building his business until he got to the point where he could quit his job. It is amazing what you can do with one less hour of sleep.

Jessica: Right.

Jim: Jessica, did you consider the timing or the economy or any other kind of external factors when you were thinking about your

146

business, how much success you might have, or what your business might even look like, or was it all "I'm going to find this need, I'm going to fill it, and it's going to be a success"?

Jessica: I did not really consider any external factors. Again, if you just look at my story on paper you'd probably think "well that probably wasn't the smartest way to do things" because I got pregnant before I knew what I was going to do for money. I mean it was probably not the smartest way to do it, but I just knew it was going to work out. Like I said, I have that dangerous optimism, and also coming from a fundraising background, a fundraiser for the past six years before the recession hit and after the recession, I was experienced in dealing with how the economy can affect your work both from a nonprofit standpoint and a business standpoint, so I didn't really let the economy be an influence. I just trained my brain to not blame things on external factors; it's just a waste of time.

Jim: I think you shared earlier that you and I had a conversation over Thanksgiving about becoming a VA and having a home-based business. So when you got started, did you seek out counsel and advice, did you read books, how did you get all the education and knowledge? The reason I'm asking this, and it seems funny that I'm asking because I know the answer: A lot of people stumble because they don't know what the first step is. "Okay, I want to be an entrepreneur, but I actually don't know what the first thing to do is." So talk about the getting started part.

Jessica: The getting started can be hard if your dad is not Jim Palmer or if you don't have that someone directing your life. Sure the answer is: I had my dad to get started and really help me lay out the goals, but there are so many things you can do. Honestly, I learned so much just from watching NewsletterGuru TV and listening to podcasts. But I think getting started is absolutely education. The difference between being an entrepreneur and having a job is you don't have someone giving you tasks – you create your own tasks, and in order to know what services and things you're going to offer people, you have to educate yourself. Reading books – I read *The Barefoot Executive* by Carrie Wilkerson and that really taught me a lot about becoming your own boss and starting your own business, but it also gave me a lot of motivation to see I wasn't the only person who wanted to stay at home, so I could be with my kids. Seeking counsel is really important; if you know someone, I think it's important that you connect with them and talk with them, but if you don't know anyone who's an entrepreneur, there are so many books you can read, there are podcasts you can listen to... you should really prioritize and invest in your own education.

Jim: I remember when you read Carrie Wilkerson's book, *The Barefoot Executive*. She really had the same mission about being a stay-at-home mom for all of her kids, so I can't say enough about books. Obviously you know I have a huge library, I'm a big fan of reading books. So for folks who might not know or don't have the resources to connect with a coach, there's a lot of education out there. You can go the library and get these books for free, or you can get Kindle versions for $7 or $8. There really is a lot of information out there. Jessica, let me ask you about the fear factor, when it comes to pulling the trigger, starting when you did. I remember when you had your last day at your "corporate job." Talk about the fear factor because that really is something that a lot of people deal with, not only starting but every day as an entrepreneur. How do you overcome the fear factor initially and do you still deal with that on occasion in the quiet moments of the night when you're working?

Jessica: Yeah, I definitely still deal with the fear factor. It's kind of ironic that I decided to become an entrepreneur and become a business owner which is, as they say, you create your own security. There's not a very comfortable job with a salary coming every week; you really need to bring in your income and create it yourself, so there's definitely a fear factor. I get scared a lot on how much money we're going to have as a family in a couple of months. At any time, a client could say, "It's not working out anymore, I don't need your services." So that is scary to think that's a reality, but as I said with the external factors, it's really important not to even focus on being afraid or the negative or external factors because you're going to be most productive, most successful when you are positive, when you're not afraid, when you're only focusing on being successful. It's all about mindset I think.

Jim: I think you're right. And you read *Think and Grow Rich* right?

Jessica: Yes

Jim: I think I told you that I'm a big fan of visualization and mind movies. Do you use mind movies to think about your successful movie and how it provides things for you? Do you do that?

Jessica: I just think about where I want my life to be and I always think about my big "why" and what I want my family life to look like with a successful business... never having to worry about finances is really why I want to grow my business. I don't want my family or my son to ever worry about how much money we have, so I really keep envisioning the future for my family, and that's really what keeps me motivated.

Jim: You said something important there – your big "why." The big "why"... if somebody is not familiar with that term... refers to something, someone or maybe even a cause that's bigger than you as an individual. So if you get really scared or feel like giving up or going to bed early or doing whatever, if you have a big "why" in your life and that's what you work for, whether it's giving back or providing for your family, you'll usually dig a little deeper, stay at work a little longer, and work a little harder for something bigger than yourself, so the big "why" is important. Let me explain a little bit about mind movies. It is very powerful because your subconscious mind doesn't know the difference between what you're thinking about as a movie, whether it's real or not. As a quick example, if you were having a nightmare that a bear was chasing you down a wooded path, you wake up in a cold sweat and your heart is racing, so your subconscious mind can't determine "is this real or not." All you know is your body reacts. So it's really powerful, especially for new entrepreneurs to always focus on positive things because that feeds your brain in a good way. What are three of your most favorite books? What are three books that you've read so far that you would recommend to new entrepreneurs?

Jessica: The first one I already mentioned, *The Barefoot Executive* by Carrie Wilkerson. It's applicable to all entrepreneurs and small business owners and people who want to be an entrepreneur. Carrie works at home to be with her kids and her story resonated with me. She really lays things out very clearly – there are chapters that she'll link to training videos you can watch. I really, really liked that book. *The Slight Edge* by Jeff Olsen is awesome – that's such a good book that really just helped me see that every little thing you do adds up to making changes in your life for better or worse. It's a really motivating book. And *Three Feet from Gold* by Greg Reed. I really liked that book because it talks about how you never know when you're three feet from gold, and I just want to tell a quick story about how right before I got my first client... after you, of course... I was getting really stressed out about money and how I knew my husband and I needed to bring in more money. I had a conference call with this individual and hadn't heard from him in a couple of days, and I was getting really nervous. I just kept telling myself I never know when I'm three feet from gold, and then I got an email from him that said, "Let's do this." He hired me as a virtual assistant, and that was three feet from gold in action. I was really stressed out, but I had no idea that an hour later, I was going to get an email that said I have a new client, so those three books really taught me a lot. And of course, *The Magic of Newsletter Marketing*, *Stick Like Glue*, and *It's OK to Be Scared But Never Give Up* are great books.

Jim: You know what's good about *Three Feet from Gold*? The story is whether you're an hour away from meeting somebody or three days away from getting a phone call or a month away from a new client, you never know how close you are, so it really speaks to perseverance. Jessica, now that you're up and running, would you say it's harder than you thought, easier than you thought or completely different than you thought?

Jessica: I think it's easier than I thought. Before I was up and running, I had no idea what to expect. The scariest thing for me as a work-at-home mom was that it wasn't just the work aspect and what I was going to be doing as a virtual assistant and what services I was going to be offering, I had no idea how I was going to manage having a newborn at home. I just couldn't even imagine it because this was my first child. So that was a really scary part for me, but I just take it day-by-day, and I keep reminding myself that every day is going to be different, the only constant is change. It is easier than I thought because I was so afraid before. But now I don't focus on that, I just focus on each positive.

Jim: If you think your business is going to look anything like you initially thought it would look, let go of that. One of the things that you're smart to do is pursue wealth creation, which means look for opportunities to provide value to other people because that's how you're going to grow your business. Some people might be unfamiliar with the term VA which stands for virtual assistant. So when we first got started, you were doing some virtual assistant work for me and then a couple of other folks. What did that look like? Explain how that works.

Jessica: Well as a virtual assistant, I offer services that help my clients' businesses run smoother and grow. As a virtual assistant for you, I do client support. When a client or prospect emails about No Hassle Newsletters or No Hassle Social Media, I help them. I help them become a client. I also do administrative work. I check the links on all the sites, so that's a lot of administrative work. But as I grew, I figured out what my strengths were, so I've turned to more social media marketing. I picked up Pinterest and realized I had a knack for it, so now I offer Pinterest marketing services to my clients. Then I started designing infographics just for fun, to kind of dabble around, and I realized "I'm really good at this and there's money in it. So let's do that." Then I also started scheduling interviews. So I figured it out, and I started doing it, and as I went, I figured out different strategies, things that made it more efficient, things that gave me more results, and I realized, again, that there was money there. There aren't a lot of people scheduling interviews on podcasts, so that was just an opportunity that I saw. As a virtual assistant, there's not one job description, it's just about offering services to entrepreneurs and business owners to help them make their business more profitable, not to be just a million different things.

Jim: I think what's important about that lesson is that you started doing some admin work, you started shipping books, you started doing client support for me. But then, I asked you about Pinterest – I'd read a little bit about it and but quite frankly I don't know too much about it. I gave you a task and said go learn about Pinterest and tell me what you learned. You came back and told me there's a lot of opportunity to use Pinterest to drive traffic to websites. And then you started creating these graphics, and it became another business. And the thing with interviews... we didn't even talk about that initially, but again you started noticing I was doing interviews, and you said, "I can get you more," and I said, "Well tell me how and let's do that." So I think the big lesson is that you kind of get started doing one thing and you branch out based on the needs of other entrepreneurs and business owners who will become your clients as a virtual assistant, so it's kind of cool. So my final question, Jess, is if you had one piece of advice to say to the readers of this book who are waiting for it to get easier, what is that one piece of advice?

Jessica: Find a mentor. We talked about this earlier in our interview and I said a couple of things that I thought about that, but it's really important that you have someone guiding you along. So if you know someone in your life who is an entrepreneur or owns a business, really connect with them. I'm lucky I have you, Dad, as an entrepreneur who has helped me along. Really get creative. If you can pay a coach, pay a coach. So many coaches have free videos, free TV shows, you will not believe how much I've learned from watching Newsletter Guru TV (www.NewsletterGuru.TV) and listening to podcasts. Read books. Really educate yourself because as a business owner, nobody's going to tell you what to do, there's no job description... you have to figure that out on your own and you've got to educate yourself in order to do that.

Jim: Awesome – great advice. Well Jessica thank you so much, and obviously I wish you so much continued success and if anybody wants to connect with you or learn more about you, what's a good website to do that?

Jessica: www.EntrepreneurSupportServices.com

Jim: Alright Jess thank you so much!

Jessica: You're welcome.

Bobby Deraco: Creating Success Where Others Failed

Jim: Thank you for being a featured guest expert in this book, Bobby, I'm excited to share an amazing story with readers. I know your story is really going to strike a cord and really close out a great section of this book because you've had such a phenomenal, kind of a rocket ship ride of growth right from the beginning. So Bobby, please take a brief moment and share just a little about who you are personally, your family and what your current business is.

Bobby: Sure, my name is Bobby Deraco. I am a father of three little girls, and I live in Lancaster, Pennsylvania. I'm only 36 years old, so certainly time and experience weren't on my side when I started my company. I can't say I like to do a whole lot other than work and hang out with my family and build businesses and spend time with my friends.

Jim: Bobby, you know when you and I first met, you were a print rep for all of the printing I was doing with No Hassle Newsletters, my books and things like that, and I want to share with our readers, that you were one of the largest, if not the largest print reps in a three- to five-year period from when you joined the company. You were like the superstar almost on a national level, and you decided to become an entrepreneur and go out on your own. Were you nervous about that? Full of energy and courage? Convinced you would be a success? Or just let's go see what happens?

Bobby: I think I thought it through pretty well. You're right – I was the number one rep out of 800 sales people in my company. Probably at the time as far as commercial printing goes, as far as volume, I was probably in the top 100 sales reps in the world as far as my industry. So to give you some key points, I was making $600,000 a year when I left. When I left, it wasn't like I was underemployed or not making any money, but what was missing for me was that I thought I could do it better, I could build a better mousetrap, I wanted a little more excitement. I had learned from my prior career that it doesn't matter how big the company you're in is, there's no better job security outside of owning your own business, and I truly believe that. I wanted to chart my own course. I didn't want to wait for somebody to come by and say, "You're making too much money, we don't need you anymore." I started five companies before that, never to the level that Synapse has become, but I kind of knew the ins and outs on a smaller level, a basic level, how businesses operate. I've always been someone who I knew if I put my mind to it, I would achieve it, so courage may be a part of it. I think honestly, I'm lucky that I didn't know too much about business; I knew just enough, but I didn't know all of the problems I would encounter. I didn't know a lot of that, and I kind of went in a little more blindly than I am now. And honestly, with three little kids, a mortgage and coming off of a fairy high maintenance life style, I knew I had to make it work. I didn't have a choice.

Jim: What's interesting is that so many entrepreneurs, Bobby, say if I knew then what I know now, I never would have started, so I think naiveté is a good thing as an entrepreneur.

Bobby: I think so too.

Jim: What was the biggest reason or motivator for launching your new business because you were already earning quite a healthy salary? Some people are probably getting out their magnifying glass and making sure they read that right on the page. I remember when you and I were talking back then – "How could we have a sales guy making this kind of money." Maybe the writing was on the wall or maybe you really wanted to take control of your destiny, as you say. And if I remember right, weren't either your parents or grandparents entrepreneurs, so you had a little bit of that in your genes, so to speak?

Bobby: Both of my grandparents had multiple businesses growing up. They were always business owners and entrepreneurs. My father has had his own businesses off and on for 30+ years, but in the last fifteen, he's sold his businesses. But you know Jim, for me it was more... I won't sugar coat it – I thought the only way I would make more money than what I was currently making was to own my own business. So that was true, although, if that was my main impetus six years ago, I can assure you today that's not what my motivation is. But if I had to give you some tangibles, I'd say, it's all relative. If I'm making $600,000 now, how can I get to a $1million? I didn't foresee that opportunity in being an employee. And at the end of the day, I think you can have a great income, but obviously I understood the difference between income and equity as well, and I really wanted to build something that was going to be of lasting value. Basically, one really scary part of it was that I was making a healthy, healthy income, but if something would have happened to me, my family would have been left with zero, so I really had to start thinking about long-term versus short-term goals and what I was going to do for my family's future and my own future.

Jim: Yeah, one of the reasons I'm so excited to interview you, Bobby, is I think there's a lot of people who are reading this book who are entrepreneurs now or maybe they are making a healthy, healthy living, but in both cases, they're struggling with "what's the next step?" And one of the reasons that I started to write this book almost six months ago, I've shared this in the early pages, I coach entrepreneurs and a couple times people said, "Yeah well, that's a good idea, but I don't think I can do that now." And I say, "Well why not?" They would say, "I'll just wait for things to get a little better." I kept hearing that over and over, and I said, "Doggone it. I have to address this and that's going to be the subject of my book." So not only did you have the courage to leave a good job and really set yourself up and your family with some ultra security other than the paycheck, but one of the reasons I'm excited to talk to you is that about two years ago, you took what was already a successful company, Synapse, and started investing in additional staff. You bought an office building for yourself, you invested in a lot of equipment because you wanted to grow that business that was already growing, and I've always been amazed that there's no lack of courage when I watch you grow your business. So let's talk about the mindset, first of all... let's paint a little bit of a picture about where you were two years ago and where you wanted to take Synapse and that kind of mindset of how you were going to get there.

Bobby: I think two years ago, between two and three years ago when I identified this, we were offering a lot of services and some of them were being bundled together based on client needs. I have an agency, a marketing firm for specifically digital and brand marketing. I had a lot of services, but they weren't wrapped overall into strategy, and I knew if I wanted to improve both our margins and improve our retention, then I had to continue to grow the services and solutions that our company offered. In the last three years, we've had three major reinventions, and I think it comes from a couple of things. Number one, you've got to move faster than the market is moving and the only way to do that is to be really face-to-face all the time with your customers. You've got to hear what your customers are struggling with; you've got to hear what their goals are and then create services, solutions and products that fit those. We were just constantly listening to what our customers were asking for and then devising new ways to do that, figuring if they were having a problem with whatever their need was, then other customers were doing that too. I didn't have a silver spoon, I never had any money, my family is not wealthy, I couldn't count on them if I screwed something up, I didn't want investors, I didn't want to go into a ton of debt. So for the last six years, I've been bootstrapping all the way. Whenever we had additional profit, I would take that and reinvest. When we'd get another client, I'd hire another person for the team. I'd buy more desks, I'd buy more computers, I'd do more marketing, so it was all bootstrapped. I never had a big investment to begin with. I was fortunate that I had some customers who enjoyed working with me that transitioned from my former career over to my company. I just think constant reinvention is key. If you call me two years from now, Jim, my company will be different than it is today. We are constantly reinventing to make sure we're staying ahead of the market as best as we can.

Jim: There's so many powerful things you said, I'm going to tick them off quickly. First of all, the power of relationships. You and I had worked together a long time at that point, and I think I was your first client at Synapse!

Bobby: I think actually the second job we did was for you; the first job was our own business cards!

Jim: That's funny. So having healthy, strong relationships is what it's all about. It's what I'm constantly preaching. The second point, Bobby, you mentioned, was listening to the pains and desires and seeing where the market's going. That's a big thing I teach, even with the newsletters, the power of "what else." What else can you help your customers with? Because once they're customers and they know, like and trust you, they're open to how you can do other things for them, so take the blinders off and stop being "Hey, I sell commodity A." Think of all the other ways you can help them. The other thing, and I can really resonate with this because it's how I've been running my business now, is constantly reinvesting the profits. Adding support staff... I know you've got thirty employees; I've got nine people who help me run my membership program and other aspects. I'm in a big transition right now with some client work we're doing. It is a little scary, and I think part of what makes us entrepreneurs is being willing to constantly reinvest in the future growth and profitability. Let me ask a question that kind of goes toward mindset: Are there regular people who you seek counsel or advice from? Other entrepreneurs?

Bobby: Over the years I've had all kinds of different approaches, Jim. I've done everything you can think of from being involved in mastermind groups, which I think are a tremendous benefit particularly if you have a good set of people that you can really bounce ideas off. I've had private consultants. I've had internal consultants that I've hired full-time. Whether those things come or go, I've always kept a couple of core principles. Number one, I've surrounded myself internally with executives who challenge my own thinking. Sometimes as a boss you get to the point where people don't ask questions, they just say yes, and I think it's important – even though sometimes it's painful to have to explain your reasoning. The whole system of having someone internally or close to you saying, "Hey why are you doing this, why aren't you doing it this way?" that's good. I think you have to have that. The second thing has always been books. Any question, any motivation that I've needed, any question I needed answered, every tough time, a solution is always written down somewhere. Every interaction I have, whether it's a prospect, a client, a vendor, a networking event, I'm always trying to pull a good idea or a good observation out of that interaction. I guess to summarize that I would say it doesn't matter how high you go on the chart, you've got to constantly be curious and humble enough to continue to grow.

Jim: Absolutely. You know, a couple of months ago I gave a talk at the Napoleon Hill Think and Grow Rich anniversary, and one of the sections of my presentation was my "Five Drivers to Big Success" and then I popped up a picture of Mr. T – and it's the one where Mr. T is nose-to-nose with Rocky and he's a lot bigger and he's got that Mohawk growing – and I said, "Everybody in here has to have a Mr. T." What that reference is, like you said, either have a coach or have executives on your team who you give permission to and expect them to hold you accountable and challenge you. Because as the owners of our businesses, we are top dog, right? I mean, if I don't want to go out and speak or I don't want to do interviews, there's nobody that's going to knock at my door and ask, "Why haven't you done that?" Because you're the owner, there's nobody higher than you. So what you have to do is always have somebody, whether they're on staff or whether they are a paid coaching position, who can say, "Hey dude, stop wimping out, get out there and start speaking" or whatever it is. That's a powerful thing, no matter how much success you have.

Bobby: Yeah, if you don't have it internally like executives in your company – if your company is not at that point or it's not your goal – definitely have a personal coach. You've got to have somebody who challenges your thinking. That's just critical, and it's never going to be your spouse.

Jim: Absolutely. Bobby, let's talk about the fear factor. That's really what it comes down to, either pulling the initial trigger or "I'm doing three grand a month and I need to be doing ten, so I've got no money. Am I going to borrow or am I just going to reinvest?" There's a lot of fears that entrepreneurs face, so when it comes time to pulling the trigger to either start a business or pull the trigger to reinvent yourself even as you're growing, what suggestions do you have? How do people overcome that fear, so they actually keep moving forward?

Bobby: I think any time you have a private company, a closely held private company or a private business, you're never going to get rid of that fear factor. There's a lot on the line. Someday when you have a fat bank account, it might be just your reputation, pride and ego. Sometimes, it's your house, collateralized against your line of credit. Sometimes it's legal issues. There's always going to be something around the corner that's scary. You've got to remember by growing and building a business, you're doing something that 99.99% of all people never attempt, so you're going to run into very particular situations where you just can't go home and call your mom, your dad, your brother, your sister, your spouse, your neighbor, your friends and talk to them about it because they won't be able to tell you much because they're not in it. I think you have to get comfortable around the fear, and for me, I think I set my own parameters. For instance, I'll give you a great example. I know how much money I need to have in my checking account for me to sleep well at night. If a banker looked at that, he would say "Bobby, you're holding on to too much cash, you're only making 1% return in your checking account and you have a 4% line of credit that you can easily pay off." So when you have somebody who's not emotionally tied to the factors of your business, sure they're going to tell you to do certain things, but you also have to have your own gut check and you have to set your own parameters. So let me tell you, if having a little bit more cash in the bank and not paying off debt keeps you sleeping well at night and helps you weather a storm, then so be it. Run your business to that point. I'll tell you another for instance. My accountant used to come and give me all of my month-end reporting on Tuesday morning at 8:00 a.m. Entrepreneurs are famous for "things are never enough." You make a couple bucks a month, you want a couple bucks more. Regardless of what my bottom line said at the end of those reports, I still had to deal with that for the rest of my business day, and it would throw my entire day off. So I asked my accountant to come over every first

Tuesday of every month at 4:00. The first thing with the fear factor is you know there's going to be stressors; find out what level of comfort you have and then make sure you have some buffer to keep those stressors out. Then moving forward, as far as growing a business, starting a business or starting a new unit of your business, I would say the best advice I can give there is plan – have a written plan, understand how you're going to analyze things from a numbers standpoint, if things are going well or things aren't. Make sure you have some fail safes in place, so this new business doesn't just fail before you know it's going downhill. I would say really keep a close eye on all aspects when it comes to growth. I think a good plan with some Plan Bs and fail safes written down and in place often gets rid of the fear because you don't just have it bouncing around in your head. You get it on paper: "This is what I'm going to do, this is what's going to happen if it doesn't work," and then it's a little more rational. And then if things do start to go south, you have a document that you can go back to and can say, "Okay, I ran out of marketing funds for this, what do I do now? I've already planned a contingency."

Jim: That's amazing. Bobby, I've got to be honest: I'm sitting here smiling because this interview is the final interview for the last section of this book, and I'm so excited to share this amazing information and content. Really, what you just gave in that answer is worth the price of the book all by itself. Do you have one or two books that are high on your must-read list that you can suggest to entrepreneurs?

Bobby: Sure, the classics, they never get old – everything from Napoleon Hill to Zig Ziglar to Harvey McKay, John Maxwell on leadership, those are all great books. I read and re-read that kind of stuff all the time. Norman Vincent Peal, Dan Kennedy's books I've read over and over. I think those are great, I've read some other great books – *Ready Fire Aim* is an excellent book that talks a lot about growing a business in different stages. I read a book called *Small by Design* which talks a lot about great businesses that don't necessarily have to be the biggest. I read a lot about psychology, and I read a lot about sales. I believe as a leader, CEO, founder or owner, your number one job is sales and marketing. I'm reading a book called *Contagious* right now which talks about why people buy. I think a lot of other things I would add, Jim... I know I spit out a lot of books, just tons of great books out there... what I would also say is one of the things that's helped me the most is to get out, be curious and have life experiences. Whether it's travel, whether it's about reading different interests, whether it's just talking to people, learning an instrument even if you're not good, taking up a sport. I've got to tell you when it goes back to building relationships with people, finding common ground and being able to take interest in somebody is important and just being curious about life around us has really helped be able to connect with a lot of people. That would be another thing, it shouldn't always be business books.

Jim: Absolutely. First of all one of the things you said is re-reading. I have a rather large 'to-be-read' pile of books, but one of the things I've started this year is re-reading some of the classics because you get so much more out of them the second or the third or maybe the fourth time you've read them.

Bobby: That's right, Jim, you see the information from a different angle, you see it five years later from a completely different perspective than what you saw five years prior.

Jim: This has been so fabulous, so let's just wrap up with this final question: If you had one piece of advice to say to the readers of this book either considering starting a business or those who already own a business but maybe are sitting on the sidelines waiting for it to get easier before they aggressively market or grow their business, what would you say to them?

Bobby: I would just say go do it. Success is 10% idea, 90% action, and honestly I'll confess something, I've never had a Plan B. I've never given myself a Plan B. I threw myself into this business and said, "Basically no matter what it takes, there might be people more experienced than me, there might be people with more capital, there might be people that have age on their side, but there will be no one, no competitor, no one in my industry who will outwork me." And I never had a Plan B; I said I was going to make this work no matter what. I think if you have that mindset, you will make it work, it's possible.

Jim: And that is phenomenal advice, and I've always believed that – whether you call it no safety net, no Plan B, I like the expression "cut the rope" – because I think when people have a Plan B, that causes them to make more conservative decisions and conservative decisions lead to conservative growth. When you go out there and really put it out there because you have no safety net, you really have to do it. You get up early, you stay later, you dig deeper, it makes you work. Let's face it, that's why they call it the top one or two percent, because 98% of the people aren't willing to do that.

Bobby: If you want something that no one else has, you have to do something no one else does – same concept.

Jim: So Bobby, I'm sure after reading this chapter, people are going to think, "I need to learn more about Bobby Deraco and his business." What's a good website, how can people go learn more about your company and connect with you?

Bobby: Sure, thanks Jim. Synapse Marketing Solutions is my business and our web address is www.synapseresults.com. They can learn all about me, my business and what we do here and connect with me on LinkedIn through there and good luck to everybody out there. I'll leave you with this Jim, I will tell you, I worked as an employee in the marketing and sales field full-time for twelve years before I started my company, and I've got to tell you, there's not one time in the past six years since I started Synapse that I've dreaded coming into work, and even if I never make a dime more than I made before, even if I make less, I have to tell you that's a pretty good handoff to spend a third of your day doing something you really enjoy, maybe half your day doing something you really enjoy and is yours. That's an outstanding

feeling, that's an awesome feeling. Even all the problems you face and all the challenges, I wouldn't trade them for where I'm at now.
Jim: And that is the final word on this book, that's awesome. Bobby you're a great friend, you're really an incredible inspiration to me and all I do in my business, so thank you very much for sharing everything you just shared.
Bobby: Likewise, I feel the same.

Stop Waiting and Get Going:

❖ Stop waiting and get busy. There's no better time than right now to either start a business or build a business that can ultimately lead to the life of your dreams.

❖ Do something even if it's wrong. You're going to learn from that.

❖ Wake up 15 minutes earlier, go to bed 15 minutes later every single day. Use those 30 minutes for nothing else but to further your education in the field that you're passionate about and that is also a viable business.

❖ Educate yourself because as a business owner, nobody's going to tell you what to do, there's no job description... you have to figure that out on your own and you've got to educate yourself in order to do that.

❖ Success is 10% idea, 90% action.

 Success Tips and Gems

You'll work harder towards success and with more determination, more willing to do 'whatever it takes' if you have no backup plan!

My good friend, Adam Urbanski told me that upon landing in America from Poland, he had little money and tore up his return flight ticket! Gutsy move but look at him today: Successful! Is there some 'safety net' that is keeping you from doing whatever it takes in your business?

"In order to succeed, your desire for success should be greater than your fear of failure." ~ Bill Cosby

"Success is not final, failure is not fatal; it is the courage to continue that counts." ~ Winston Churchill

Chapter Thirteen: Lessons Learned

The most important lesson, and the one I hope you learned by the end of Chapter 1 or 2 is that *now is the best time* to launch your business or, if you are already running your business, it's the best time to pull the trigger to take the next step and jump into the next phase of your enterprise. The only thing waiting does is delay your success and your ability to create your own personal economic boom.

Thomas Edison learned to trust his vision about how electricity could change the world, and Bill Gates learned the exact same thing about his vision of a computer on every desk and in every household. In retrospect, they might have both underestimated the results, but nevertheless, both became wildly successful. Bill Hewlett and Dave Packard may not have had such lofty visions at the start of their enterprise, but they learned how to take the blinders off and follow the money.

Media magnates Henry Luce and Ted Turner both launched enterprises in tough times and scoffed at naysayers. Pay a dollar for *Fortune* in 1929? A news channel that never went off the air? Seemed like crazy talk at the time, but today we know better. We can certainly learn from their confidence about their respective products and desire to succeed.

Cosmetics, an unarguable luxury, proved to be anything but during the Great Depression and again during the recent Great Recession. Consumers wanted it their way as the Burger King founders quickly learned, and like round-the-clock news, pancakes all day wasn't a crazy idea either. Find a desire and fill it, and you'll pave your own path to success.

Be like Fed Ex's Fred Smith – think outside the box, find a better way, and be persistent. He saw that existing air freight routes were neither effective nor efficient. According to entrepreneurial legend, at a time when he was losing millions a week, he literally gambled to make payroll, and one of his pilots purportedly charged aviation fuel on his own personal credit card. Smith would not be deterred from his idea. He (and his employees) understood the importance of GPS – guts, persistence, and strategy – to ensure that a great idea evolved into an undeniable success.

Technology then, technology now. Video may not have really killed the radio star, but that alteration in the way we use technology changed the way we perceive and consume music. And MTV started way, way back in technological stone age of 1981, before the Digital Revolution really got underway. How can you use today's technology to create your empire?

The bottom line to any business success is to fill a need or desire, find a better way to do things, solve problems and ease pain, offer value at every turn, and open your mind to dream about the possibilities. With that formula, there is never a bad time to launch a business, so stop waiting!

Cut the Rope

Starting a small business takes a lot of guts, and there's one more strategy that I'd like to share with you and that many of the entrepreneurs I interviewed discussed. I call it cutting the rope. Others might call it not having a 'Plan B'!

However you describe it, I believe that your chances of succeeding are far better if you 'go all in.' If you have a 'Plan B' or safety net of some kind, then, when it comes time to make the hard choices or do the hard things entrepreneurs need to do, it will be too easy for you to avoid doing them. Avoiding them will absolutely limit or even undermine your success.

I want to share a bit of a history lesson with you that John Lee Dumas mentioned to me that will help you understand the importance of no Plan B and its effect on mindset.

The year was 1519, and Hernán Cortés landed on a vast plateau called Mexico. He had with him about 600 Spaniards sans protective armor, roughly 16 horses and fewer than a dozen boats. He also had a dream of conquering an empire that contained some of the world's greatest treasure, including gold, silver, and precious Aztec jewels. By logical standards, the attempt to conquer such an extensive empire signaled that Cortés possibly also had a death wish.

You see, for more than 600 years, other conquerors with far greater resources who had attempted to colonize Mexico and take the treasure failed. Cortés knew the history and knew of previous failed attempts, so he took a different approach in his quest to conquer the Aztecs.

Instead of charging ahead and forcing his men into immediate battle, Cortés remained on the beach and and worked to inspire his men with stirring speeches. He urged the spirit of adventure and stoked the desire for lifetimes of fortune. In coaching mastery, he turned a military exercise into an adventure in the minds of his troops. Through all of his oratories, it was a matter of three words that changed the history of the New World. Cortés ordered, **"Burn the boats."**

It was a command that smacked of lunacy: If defeat loomed at the hands of the Aztecs, there was no exit strategy... no way to retreat... no way to save their lives. There was no Plan B. Cortés was "all in."

Rather than undermining the confidence of his men, it had the opposite effect. With only two choices, ensure victory or die, it ignited the will to win. The outcome is recorded in history: Hernán Cortés became the first man in 600 years to successfully conquer Mexico.

There's some dispute about the veracity of this story, but it's not difficult to believe. A move like this would have (and very likely did) change the mindset of the men fighting for Cortés. With no way out and the healthy survival instinct innate in each of us, victory resulted.

Knowing what you now know about mindset, it's time for you to take the same action that Cortés did to conquer Mexico and ultimately enjoy riches beyond belief: Burn your boats. Cut whatever rope you might see as an escape lifeline. Put Plan B in the shredder. Those actions will create the mindset you need to be successful.

Stop Waiting and Get Going:

❖ Without a doubt, now is the best time to launch your business or take the next big step. Mega-successful and now famous entrepreneurs started in shaky, if not downright frightening, economies. Economy isn't an excuse. Just the opposite – it's a great reason.

❖ Believe in your idea and employ GPS.

❖ Burn your boats and shred any Plan B. With no ability to retreat, you'll set your mind on forward progress and success!

 Success Tips and Gems

Leaders are not dull! Being at the top of your entrepreneurial game – 'The Sharpest Knife in the Drawer' – requires a mindset that seeks constant improvement, always honing your competitive edge. Sharp leaders do the hard work every day that others refuse to do and continuously invest in their future by surrounding themselves with even sharper leaders!

"Most of the important things in the world have been accomplished by people who have kept on trying when there seemed to be no hope at all." ~ Dale Carnegie

"Sometimes when you innovate, you make mistakes. It is best to admit them quickly, and get on with improving your other innovations." ~ Steve Jobs

"Burn the boats." ~ Hernán Cortés

Lessons Learned

Chapter Fourteen: Stop Waiting – What to Do Now

If you've made it this far in the book, congratualtions! Did you know that most people never make it past the first third of a book?

I'll take the fact that you are still reading as a sign that you've been inspired from this book (which makes me very happy!) and are serious about starting a new business or getting aggressive about growing a business you've already started. If that's true, the let me say for a second time, congratualtions! You might be wondering what to do now. Here are a few thoughts for you.

1. I strongly urge you to consider hiring a coach and/or joining a mastermind group. Both of these may feel like you're putting the cart before the horse and while that would be a somewhat normal reaction – you would be wrong. Hiring a coach or joining a mastermind is investing in your future growth and profitability. More than any other investment, this will dramatically accelerate your growth and success.

2. Do as much research as possible on your vision, idea, or passion. Ah, passion! Let me address passion. I do believe that when you're passionate about something that's a good thing and will generally help to make you work harder and be more focused. However, simply being passionate about something does not mean it will make a profitable business. Regardless of your passion

for your business idea, there must be a 'need' for it in order for you to create a profitable business.

This question will illustrate what I just mentioned about passion: If you wanted to open a successful and profitable restaurant and you had your choice of three 'wish list' items, which one would you choose?

- The best location,
- The best chef, or
- The best and friendliest wait staff?

Actually, it's a trick question because the most important thing for a restaurant to be successful is a starving, hungry crowd! You see, no matter how passionate you are about your secret recipes, and no matter if you find the best location, chef, and wait staff… if there aren't enough people 'hungry' for what you offer, you will not succeed.

3. Take action. The first step is the hardest, but nothing helps to alleviate fear like action. Don't think about the thousands of steps in front of you – only think about step one and get it done. With that complete, then you can think about the next step.

4. Start a steady diet of information and success training. This includes reading books, watching videos, attending seminars, etc. Fortunately for you, I offer a ton of free training through Newsletter Guru TV, Stick Like Glue Radio, and my weekly newsletters -- all free! I also encourage you to read my other books and candidily will say that all of this will be the best education you can receive on how to build a more profitable business faster! Go to www.TheNewsletterGuru.com and put your name and email in the box you'll find in the upper

right side – I'll reward you with some instant bonuses and then you'll also be able to take advantage of my free weekly training.

5. Finally, if you liked and appreciated the information in this book, I'd like to ask you to help me get it in the hands of other people like you. The best and easiest way to do this would be to post a review on Amazon. Thank you in advance for your five-star review!

I'm going to end this book by sharing what I call my "Big Drivers of Success." I was honored to share these with an audience at the Napoleon Hill Think and Grow Rich Summit in April 2013:

Have a burning desire to play a bigger game: "Desire is the starting point of all achievement." A burning desire will get you out of bed earlier, make you work harder and dig deeper when times are tough.

Serve first – be a giver: Five Important Words: "How can I serve you?" This is a great mantra for any business.

Treat customers like family, or better: Your customers are not an interruption in your day – they are the reason you have a business.

Always operate with integrity. Period.

Give back and have a "Big Why": Why do you do this? I believe in life and business that we reap what we sow. I encourage you to be a giver – give your time and give back as you succeed. In my videos, I often call this planting seeds. If you want to reap a big harvest, you need to be always planting a lot of seeds.

"The best time to plant a tree was 20 years ago. The second best time is now." ~ Chinese proverb

Finally, after writing this entire book, just the other day I heard an old Chinese Proverb that just about sums up my entire main message!

The best time to plant a tree was 20 years ago.
The second best time is now!

So there you have it! I hope by now you are inspired and believe what I do – that NOW is the perfect time to start creating your dream business. Undertsand that fear is normal and most likely won't go away. Let this fear energize you, and in every action you take, you'll be one step close to kicking this fear to the curb. I wish you all the success you dream about and please email me at guru@thenewsletterguru.com to let me know about your business and success.

Stop Waiting and Get Going:

❖ Don't fall into the trap of believing that hiring a coach or joining a mastermind group is putting the cart before the horse. It will pave the way to your success.

❖ Passion alone will not create a profitable business. There must be a need. Be sure the need is there first.

❖ Take action. Don't hesitate to start because there seems to be too many steps. Take a step and begin.

❖ Continue learning. Become a voracious consumer of information and success training.

 Success Tips and Gems

"A journey of a thousand miles begins with a single step." ~ Lao-tzu, Chinese philosopher

"Whatever the mind of man can conceive and believe, it can achieve." ~ Napoleon Hill

"Your time is limited, so don't waste it living someone else's life." ~ Steve Jobs

About the Author – Jim

Learn More About Jim:

Jim's other books:

The Magic of Newsletter Marketing—The Secret to More Profits and Customers for Life

Stick Like Glue – How to Create an Everlasting Bond with Your Customers So They Stay Longer, Spend More, and Refer More!

The Fastest Way to Higher Profits – 19 Immediate Profit-Enhancing Strategies You Can Use Today

It's Okay to Be Scared But Never Give Up (with Martin Howey)

Check out Jim's wildy popular Smart Marketing and Business Building Programs:

No Hassle Newsletters – www.NoHassleNewsletters.com

No Hassle Social Media – www.NoHassleSocialMedia.com

Newsletter Guru TV – www.NewsletterGuru.TV

Stick Like Glue Radio – www.GetJimPalmer.com

Jim's Concierge Print and Mail on Demand Program – www.newsletterprintingservice.com

Double My Retention – www.DoubleMyRetention.com

Custom Article Generator - www.customarticlegenerator.com

No Hassle Inforgraphics - www.nohassleinfographics.com

Jim's Mastermind and Private Coaching – www.TheNewsletterGuru.com

The Magnetic Attraction and Retention System (MARS Training Program) – www.MarsTrainingProgram.com

Jim's Free Weekly Newsletter – www.JimsNewsletter.com

Interested in hiring or learning more about Jim? Visit www.TheNewsletterGuru.com

About Jim

Jim Palmer is a marketing and business building expert and host of Newsletter Guru TV and Stick Like Glue Radio. He is known internationally as 'The Newsletter Guru' – the go-to resource for maximizing the profitability of customer relationships. He is the founder and President of Custom Newsletters, Inc., parent company of No Hassle Newsletters, No Hassle Social Media, The Newsletter Guru's Concierge Print and Mail on Demand, Magnetic Attraction and Retention Training Program (MARS), Success Advantage Publishing, Double My Retention, No Hassle Infographics, and Custom Article Generator.

Jim is the acclaimed author of

- *The Magic of Newsletter Marketing – The Secret to More Profits and Customers for Life*
- *Stick Like Glue – How to Create an Everlasting Bond With Your Customers So They Spend More, Stay Longer, and Refer More*
- *The Fastest Way to Higher Profits – 19 Immediate Profit-Enhancing Strategies You Can Use Today*
- *It's Okay To Be Scared – But Don't Give Up* – A book of hope and inspiration for life and business
- *Stop Waiting for it to Get Easier – Create Your Dream Business Now!*

Jim was also privileged to be a featured expert in *The Ultimate Success Secret*; *Dream, Inc.*; *ROI Marketing Secrets Revealed*; *The Barefoot Executive*; and *Boomers in Business*.

Jim Palmer speaks and gives interviews on such topics as newsletter marketing, client retention, entrepreneurial success, the fastest way to higher profits, how to use social media marketing and how to achieve success in business.

Jim is a cancer survivor, has been married for thirty-three years, has four grown children and a grandson. He lives in Chester County, Pennsylvania with his wife, Stephanie, their cat, Linus, and Toby, the marketing dog. Jim and Stephanie love to kayak, travel, and spend time with their family.

Connect with Jim on Facebook, Twitter, Google+, LinkedIn®, and tune into his Web TV show.

For more resources and information on Jim, his blog, and his companies, visit www.NewsletterGuru.tv.

To get your copy of Jim's free weekly newsletter, *More Profits and Customers for Life,* visit www.JimsNewsletter.com.

BONUS OFFER

There's Not a Business on the Planet That Can't Benefit Big Time from a Monthly Customer Newsletter!

And My Wildly Popular "No Hassle" Newsletter Program Makes it Easy as 1-2-3!

If you're one of the many entrepreneurs or small business owners who struggle producing a newsletter so much so that your monthly newsletter only goes out ... 3 to 4 times per year, then you must try No Hassle Newsletter and my famous "Customer-Loving™" content. With No Hassle Newsletters your customer newsletter can be done in about 23 minutes or less! Guaranteed!

Join **No Hassle Newsletters** today and after you do, send an e-mail to guru@TheNewsletterGuru.com telling me that you joined because of this book, and I'll send you a **certificate good for one FREE newsletter critique—value $795!**

Free Marketing and Business-Building Information Reveals the Secret to Boosting Your Profits Now!

Get immediate access to valuable marketing and business-building information that will help you significantly boost your profits by getting more repeat and referral business!

- **TWO CHAPTERS FREE:** Get the first 2 chapters of three of my hit books: *The Magic of Newsletter Marketing, Stick Like Glue,* and *The Fastest Way to Higher Profits!*
- **FREE PROFIT BOOSTING VIDEO:** "The Power of Zero" will show you how to explode the growth of your business!
- **FREE MONEY MAKING REPORT:** "Don't Be A Newsletter Pansy, aka Use Newsletters And Grow Rich!"